THE CRY OF A LITTLE BOY

Overcoming "The Struggle"

Tracy J. Sipp

PublishAmerica
Baltimore

First printing

ISBN: 1-4137-2174-5
PUBLISHED BY
PUBLISHAMERICA, LLLP.
www.publishamerica.com
Baltimore

Printed in the United States of America

This book is dedicated to the incredible women who have graced my life:

- My baby sister, Gwendolyn P, Sipp, who was also my precious angel (Feb. 9, 1964 – Aug. 27, 1994).
- My mother, Geneva O. Sipp, who like most mothers did the very best she knew how to do when it came to loving her children.
- My sister, Lisa L. Adams, who has always protected and loved me unconditionally. She is also the kind of mother that most children would dream of having.
- Aunt Edith Payne, the lady who encouraged me as a child and as a teenager to follow my dreams despite how different I was.

IN MEMORY

Elbert B. Sipp, Father
(Oct. 1997 – Deceased)

Jeffrey L. Sipp, Brother
(Aug. 1995 – Deceased)

Gregory G. Sipp, Brother
(July 1993 – Deceased)

Norris Robinson, Best Friend
(Dec. 1999 – Deceased)

ACKNOWLEDGEMENTS

I would like to take this opportunity to acknowledge several individuals who helped inspire me in some way to write this book, or who have supported me during the most difficult times of my life. First and foremost, I give honor to my Lord and Savior, Jesus Christ, for giving me the wisdom, power, boldness, and courage, to write this book and for giving me a second chance. I would also like to again acknowledge my baby sister, the late Gwendolyn P. Sipp, who I also dedicate my book to. I thank her for allowing me to find purpose living through the fantasy of her life. I acknowledge my mother, Geneva O. Sipp, a woman full of courage, strength, love, and over comer of challenges. I give thanks as well to my sister, Lisa L. Adams, who never judged me and for always giving from her heart. I would be amiss if I did not acknowledge my deceased father, Elbert B. Sipp, and brothers, Jeffrey L. and Gregory G. Sipp; may you rest in peace.

I certainly want to give many thanks to Oprah Winfrey and Dr. Maya Angelou, both great women, who continue to encourage people all over the world. Through their gifts and talents, they both have encouraged and helped me get through the struggles that threatened my life. I especially honor them for the tremendous work they do through their medium on exposing child abusers and predators. To former NBA star, Magic Johnson, for being a true role model in his fight against the HIV/AIDS virus, and for being a living example of courage. To E. Lynn Harris, a wonderful author who, through his books, has encouraged me to pour out my heart in this my first book.

H. Patrick Eugene, a young man who defines brotherhood and friendship; one I respect so greatly that I consider him to be my adopted brother. Bishop Alfred and Co-Pastor Susie Owens, my first spiritual parents, thank you for touching the core of my soul by teaching me the gospel and for leading me to salvation through Jesus Christ.

To Pastors Edgar and Anne Mack, my current pastors who have been diligent about watching and praying for my soul, you are truly pastors after God's own heart.

To all of the following preachers who I have partnered with, Joyce Meyers, Bishop T. D. Jakes, Bishop Eddie Long, Dr. Creflo Dollar, Pastor Widley Jackson, Bishop James Morton, Pastor Charles Stanley, and Bishop Noel Jones.

To the staff at Grady Memory Healthcare Hospital, thank you all for helping me back to recovery with dignity. I'd also like to thank my first personal doctor, Joyce Drayton, M.D., who treated me with respect and dignity at the Morehouse Medical Staff Clinic.

Benjamin Dortch, Jr., and the Dortch family, I thank you for the love and support you have given me over the years. Sister Diane DeMary, thank you for going the extra mile for a stranger and for opening your home when I didn't have anywhere to go while I was very ill. To Kimberly Leach, Paula Molden, Lisa Wu Sweat, Carol Morrow, My Play Mother Carrie Biscoe, Michael Harper, Michael Kittrell, Sharon Richardson, Freda Richardson, Shan Jordan, Saxton Sayble, Lee Johnson, Renetta Flemmings and Minister Andriette Turner I appreciate your friendships and you being a listening ear. Special thanks to my church family, SOTW Sword of The

Word Evangelistic Church in East Point, GA. For the late Norris Robinson, for everything I would ever need to know regarding HIV/AIDS, and for the many others who prayed my strength in the Lord; you know who you are.

To my book confidant, Minister Wendy Barber, who I have recently met; while certainly my book could have been possible had someone else accepted the job, God knew you would be the one who'd experience my life along with me and help me convey the full struggles and pains I've experienced. I appreciate how you took on this job with resilience and passion, and for sharing along with me my tears, pain, struggles, and celebrations. For these things, I will always be grateful to you. Finally, to the many people and homosexuals who can identify with the hardships of my life, I thank you for reading my work.

PROLOGUE

The words you are about to read will take you on a journey like you've never been before. I promise at times you will be awed by the utter horrors that were inflicted upon me by those who have so adversely affected my life. I pray that while reading this book, you are not hit too hard; all I ask is that you allow your spirit and heart to open to my life story. I realize that many of you who are about to read my story have never had to understand the struggles of homosexuality. I also realize that there are still others who flatly refuse to allow themselves to understand or accept those struggling with this demon. My hope is that by reading with an open mind, you all will begin to understand what so many homosexuals struggle to overcome; in particular what my challenges have been over my 40 years of life. Most, this book shows that because God resides in each one of us, we are able to persevere and overcome all obstacles we face from day to day. After reading this book, you should feel confident that you can stand alone when no one else understands or identifies with you; that if you rely on God, he will be your strength no matter how dark your days seem. My desire is to get you to know that when everyone else says you can't, God says you can!

THE STRUGGLE BEGINS

Can you imagine a little boy about five years old living in a world full of confusion because he doesn't understand what sexuality has to do with his innocent life? He always knew he was different; how else could he explain the cruel teasing he was forced to endure at the hands of children and adults in his community. This teasing was always about his questionable sexuality; one that spelled homosexuality in the minds of those around him. To make matters worse, this little boy also endured years of pain caused from being repeatedly molested by his older brother, men as old as his father, and young boys from the around neighborhood. These relentless acts of torment and molestation would eventually cause him to suffer from a sexual addiction so damning that it would ultimately bring him to the brink of destruction, almost resulting in an untimely death.

My name is Tracy J. Sipp, and the little boy you are about to read about is me. For many years I reflected over my life as far back as age five and wondered how I got to this point and what purpose God ultimately had for my life. The horrendous events of my life haunted me every day for many years because of the guilt and shame I carried due to the many dark secrets I kept inside about my childhood and the sexual assaults I was forced to endure at the hands of others. I have never shared my life with others because I felt responsible for much of the pain that was inflicted on me as a child. I, like most children of abuse, never wanted to blame anyone or cause shame to my family for the life I had been dealt. I thought that if I just kept things quietly to myself the horrors would all go away, allowing me to move on with my life. I tried to look forward to a better life, but the better life I looked forward to never came. Instead of vanishing, my pains and secrets ended up being stored deep down within my soul, only to rise up later in ways I would live to regret.

As a little boy I was constantly reminded by those in my surroundings that it was I who was the problem because of the abnormal way I looked and the effeminate way I tended to act. The more I tried to hide this abnormal behavior, the more it would appear. Many days and nights were spent with me practicing how to be the little boy I so badly wanted to be, but unfortunately a change never resulted. In fact, my name alone was a constant indication of how different I was. Although most people said the name Tracy could be used for boy or girl most people related it to that of a girl in the same way that I did. I always wanted a masculine name like John or Chase; anything that had a "manly" sound to it. There were many days that I hated my very existence. Not only did I not want to show my face to the world but I would sometimes pray to have all my pain erased by death. I often sat and thought about my sexuality and how much hatred was shown to little boys who obviously were different from normal little boys. I could never understand why I was so different and why so much attention was shown towards me; after all I was only a little boy. I sought answers from others and even from God, yet I still didn't receive any answers. While some people struggled to figure out what made me so different, the thing they knew for sure was that my certain type of uniqueness would not be tolerated or accepted. I even sought out answers that would not come for many years, at least not until I came to understand that homosexuality was at the root of my problem. While some did openly label me a homosexual, others would just see me as a freak. As a child I was clueless to what a homosexual was. While most people made much fun of the little five-year-old boy, I struggled to find ways to deal with the differences that defined me and the pain that the molestations caused. Becoming the comic and jokester was my attempt to cope with those things I had trouble enduring, but in the end the joke was always on me because my inner struggles never subsided.

Today, I spend a lot of time thinking about children who endured the same pain I experienced. Most of my life I have wondered how an innocent child such as I was at age five could be born into a world so full of sin. Some know and understand early in their lives what God intends for them, but for others like me we struggle to uncover life's intentions for us. It seems that my life has always been a struggle because I have always battled to understand the life of a homosexual. The reason I use the word "struggle" is because this one word best describes what I have spent most of my life in. It would not be until I reached adulthood that I would begin to understand the purpose for my life and what my struggle was all about. I would understand that my struggle was much bigger than me and certainly something I would never be able to handle on my own. I had to learn the hard lesson in life which is that we are nothing without God, and only God can provide us with the true purpose we all are uniquely born to fulfill. Our struggles belong to God because he alone can remove them. Unfortunately, I wouldn't learn that lesson until I was forty years old. Up to that point I would force myself to try and fight this battle on my own.

It has always felt like my mind and body were consumed by a stronghold or were held in bondage; oppressed by locks and chains that have caused me to suffer many years of depression. Much of my depression stemmed from my childhood memories, and would cause a devastating life journey at the hands of those who would never understand me or try to walk in my shoes. As I grew older, I began to try to make adjustments to myself but nonetheless the hatred continued and at times got worse. I wondered what had caused such hatred from a community who supposedly knew nothing about me or the homosexual lifestyle. I particularly could not understand why those who brought me pain through raping my body and stealing my soul had such a lack of compassion. How the older men and boy perpetrators lived two lives, one that showed them to be upstanding in the community and the other that allowed them to harm me in hidden places and in the dark. It would be almost too late for my life before I realized what their hatred was all about and how I had allowed it to almost destroy me. I searched the world looking for answers that no one would be able to provide. For me there would never be a polite way to explain the life of a homosexual in such a way that it would cause the world to find compassion for us. Even with the many crises that the world faces today homosexuals still face an unyielding ridicule. Even though many homosexuals will lose their lives to death because of suicide, disease, and abuse, still no love can be found for them. From childhood straight into my adult life I fought to be understood by an uncompassionate world. One of the greatest lessons I've learned in life is that my struggle has always been beyond my control and certainly out of my will.

I, like many other homosexuals, have always wanted to tell my story about what we endure in the world and especially within the walls of the church. However, many years before I accepted Christ into my life I only knew to accept the disgust that outsiders share for the homosexual. For the past eleven years of my life I have struggled at even being faithful to God. I've been committed to church, and I have observed that many still had no compassion for the homosexual. I've listened to preachers and churchgoers who continually preached their favorite sermon on how all homosexuals were going to hell. I guess I have one such minister to thank for sharing her ignorance in such a way that it caused me to begin writing this book.

One night in March 2003, while attending my church yearly anniversary program, I had the opportunity to hear a guest evangelist deliver a sermon which went far beyond rebuking homosexuality, it actually bordered on verbally abusing those who suffered from this affliction. Her insults were so strong that it not only insulted me but I later learned that it had insulted some of the straight members of the church. It was very apparent that this evangelist had drawn a clear line in the sand and separated homosexuality from every other sin and hailed it as the worse sin anyone could ever commit. I was not bothered by the fact that her sermon informed the congregation that homosexuality is sin, because I understood that this doctrine came from the word of God as expressed in the Bible. However, after hearing her bash the homosexual for three nights, I began to understand what disturbed me about her words. I could not believe how this "woman of God" continued to preach on and on about how she personally hated homosexuals and men who perpetrated the act. As a representative of God I was in total disbelief, because Christians are supposed to do as Christ did. While she did speak against other sinful acts, no other caused her to spew hatred like that of homosexuality. This evangelist was honest about her past as she shared with the congregation how she had been a madam of prostitutes and a drug dealer before she accepted her call to the ministry. Somehow she didn't see her past sins in the same light as the sin of being involved intimately with the same sex. Her arrogance ignited something in me that made me want to defend this wrong, and with that I began to write my feelings down. What began as my direct response to this evangelist's misguided prejudice became a flood of feelings that led me to tell my story and to express why we must never inflict pain on others. As I began to write a response to this evangelist's attack on the homosexual, I soon identified the church as an unwilling part of the problem. As I began to write, I came to understand that there were many correlations between the lack of compassion in society, the continuing pain inflicted on these social outcasts, and the feeling of helplessness the church faces on how to help them. So began the dilemma I uncovered as I began writing from my heart.

JUDGMENT DAY

There are those who cheer the bashing of God's children; those children who struggle with the fight against the spirit of homosexuality. Ignorance has always been an easy excuse for them to target the homosexual, but God encourages us to read and study his word in order to learn how to accept people struggling with personal demons. Most importantly, it is the responsibility of those who have been chosen to pastor or minister not to stand before their congregation and victimize the struggling homosexual in particular. God sees us all the same, and therefore does not see one sin as being more deplorable than another. To God sin is sin.

Indeed, the spirit of homosexuality is an abomination to God. However, please keep in mind that it is a spirit like any other sinful spirit that the church may face. We, like God, should hate all sin and while hating the sinfulness of homosexuality is biblically correct, having a personal hate against those struggling with it is just as sinful in God's eyes. Homosexuals want to enjoy a church foundation like anyone else, and passing judgment on them is wrong and God isn't pleased with so-called Christians who sit in judgment of others. The Bible shows us time and time again that God takes no pleasure in those who commit personal attacks against individuals struggling with afflictions. In this regard, using derogatory and inflammatory names against the homosexual such as "FAGGOT" is not biblical! The term homosexual is the correct biblical name for one who involves themselves sexually with the same gender.

Because homosexuality is a sin in which most churches can't or don't deal with, many church folk believe using names like faggot is fine. I believe this is because the spirit of homosexuality is depicted in the Bible as a sin offensive to God. However, the Bible also says that while God hates the sin he loves the sinner. The dictionary cites the word "Faggot" as: a name used disparagingly against a male homosexual. The word "disparagingly" means: degrade, below one's class; lower in rank or reputation; depreciate by indirect means; and speak slightingly about. Our God would not condone using these kinds of demeaning references toward a soul. The words: faggot, sissy, and punk, are used solely to continue to belittle homosexuals in the way that the word Nigger is meant to demean the African American. These are very hateful words which God is not pleased with.

Christians are taught to reach others through LOVE, especially those who have been called as leaders in the ministry. In order to help those struggling to be delivered from any sin or sinful lifestyle, we as Christians are to continue to seek God's direction so that we might become more pleasing in God's sight. Because we all battle sin, there is no one group of people who is better than another. We are all in a spiritual battle against the sins of the enemy. Since the beginning of Christianity judgmental churchgoers within the Body of Christ have judged homosexuals as a group of weak individuals who defiantly want to be something other than what God has made them. Let's be clear, all homosexuals do not desire to be females, and surely all homosexuals are not sexual predators preying on men or boys because of an uncontrollable sexual perversion. This is where the ignorance begins.

It is very important to create a dialogue about homosexuality, especially within the church. Please keep in mind that the spirit of homosexuality is a powerful spirit and the body of Christ must begin to understand that those with this spirit are in a spiritual warfare.

Everything begins with education, and it is the obligation of spiritual leaders to help teach their members the truth about the spirit of homosexuality, otherwise hatred will continue being generated throughout the church due to ignorance. It is shameful that in 2003, the church is still hiding and has not allowed itself to get to the root of this demonic spirit. While ignorance within the church is still allowed in this area, we are losing thousands of souls to death because this topic is not acceptable to talk about in the house of God. Pastors and other spiritual leaders are still unwilling to learn how this spirit affects so many souls, therefore we will always have a hell bound group of individuals searching for freedom and feeling worthless due to living a life away from God's will. By continuing to avoid this issue and allowing the ignorance of this spirit to remain concealed, many innocent individuals including family members continue to suffer.

It is disheartening to think that homosexuals are the only group of people who are never expected to discuss their struggles, hurts, or pains, because heterosexuals are not open to hearing about their life challenges. Other types of addictions are acceptable to the heterosexual, including addictions to drugs, heterosexual sex, alcohol, prostitution, gambling, and others. It has become part of our culture to provide addiction programs which help recovering addicts in these areas, but there still remains little help or acceptance for the homosexual. When discussing homosexuality, it is clear to see that it is the only form of addiction that does not receive the same compassion that is extended to those battling other addictions.

It has been said by some ministers, pastors, and other spiritual leaders, that those struggling with the spirit of

19

homosexuality should not be allowed to function in key leadership positions in the church. My question to them is this: Should Christians struggling with other sinful spirits be allowed to be used by God? If not, then who would be left to do the work within the Body of Christ? The Bible tells us that no one is perfect enough to throw the first stone.

In reading the Bible one learns that many prophets and other significant individuals struggled with sinful behaviors and still went on to be very powerful representatives for God. Although these biblical figures struggled with their personal sins every day, God never turned his back on them in the way Christians do today. One must know that the Holy Spirit chooses to use whomever he pleases; no human being is in control of who the Holy Spirit chooses to use.

Remember God is both judge and jury and thank God that he opens up his arms to all who want deliverance through Christ. I encourage you to be like God. Open up your arms to those who are struggling with personal demons, don't judge but pray for them, because until we can learn to love and pray sincerely for others, humanity as a whole will continue to suffer and God Almighty will continue to turn his face away from us. Love covers a multitude of sin; God said it…if only we could take the time to practice it!!!

THE MOLESTATION OF INNOCENCE

Let me say this up front, I am not condoning homosexuality. As a 40-year-old male, I have struggled with this sinful spirit since childhood. I don't expect anyone who has never struggled with this demonic spirit to understand my struggle, but I do expect the same grace and mercy that is extended to others dealing with their own personal sins. There are thousands of suffering individuals who refuse to go to church because they are ridiculed as they struggle with the spirit of homosexuality. These individuals are made to feel worthless by those in the world and Christians churchgoers alike. I agree that we should frown on all sin, but all sin must include more than the sin of homosexuality. It is not uncommon for churches to offer support groups for different addictions. In fact, they have created various church axillaries that assist drug abusers, convicts, and the homeless. Most recently, some churches have even implemented HIV/AIDS ministries because of the effect this disease has had on women and children. Still most churches refuse to address the spirit of homosexuality by offering help to men and women who struggle in this area. This is not to say that a few churches don't offer compassion; however, the church at large refuses to address and acknowledge the spirit of homosexuality because many are afraid or embarrassed to discuss it. As with anything we don't accept or understand, it is far easier to make fun of it. From the pulpit it is easy to pick apart those who struggle with the spirit of homosexuality because of the level of hatred in the church for this sin. Please keep in mind that when a pastor, minister, or leader, encourages such hatred within the Body of Christ it serves to separate the body because of ignorance. Such strong hatred for the spirit of homosexuality perpetuates more hatred towards this part of the body than with any other sin. I encourage that more love be shown to all sinners, so that all might know the love of Jesus Christ. I encourage that more prayer be directed towards the homosexual so that all might be delivered from this bondage. Through prayer and biblical teaching all sinners can have a transformed life that is pleasing to God.

When a person is in bondage and can't find help, they continue to hide. This often causes them harm and/or causes them to harm others. In other words, when people are not sure of how to deal with inner turmoil they are sure to go in hiding which will surely cause them more harm. Others can be harmed as well when homosexuals feel forced to hide, especially when a homosexual feels that the only way to hide their affliction is by marrying an innocent person; they believe that this action will make them appear normal to others.

With the spread of the HIV/AIDS virus and other sexual transmitted diseases there needs to be time out for promoting ignorance and instead begin offering viable support to all people. As a man servant to God, it is my prayer to see a change in the Christian community and see a move towards the church helping to educate the Body of Christ with love, so that we may set many people free from the spirit of homosexuality and from the ignorance that is caused by fear of it.

Many homosexuals are very confused individuals, who like any other human being want love and to be loved. Many homosexuals struggle with this difficult spirit and are often angry people who are not sure of how to deal with this complex issue in their lives. Added pressure from ignorant people only make them feel worthless, which in turn causes them to continue to hide behind personal pain; and we know what some people do when they feel threatened or hated. They fight back! Many homosexuals often suffer with social anxiety disorder because of not being accepted by society. For myself, I believe that my anxiety disorder began around age five when people began teasing and calling me unpleasant names. The names people called me were the usual—Faggot, Funny, Sissy, Punk, etc. I was not only teased by other children and my siblings, but by adults as well. This caused me to run away and hide from the world; which stunted my ability to learn to interact in the real world. While being called these painful names I also felt unyielding confusion because I didn't have a clue as to why I was being verbally abused.

To be honest, even at that young age, I did know deep down inside that I was different from other little children. I spent much of my time as a little child trying to figure out what made me so different. I was so afraid of being around people for fear of being judged. As a child I found comfort just being in my room and hiding in closets just so I didn't have to be around people. Also as a child I faced harassment on a daily basis while going to school and during after school programs. This had a huge impact on my self-confidence, which in turn stripped me of my self-esteem; something I lack even to this day. As a very "different" child things only got worse as I got older.

I can recall in elementary school being treated much like the little girls because of my shyness and less masculine physical traits. I could not explain why I looked so much like a little girl, but I did easily identify with them. Children around me certainly didn't have a problem reminding me of just how much they opposed my behavior, since I was in fact a little boy. I felt very confused as a child because I didn't understand

23

why there was so much criticism from other little children and adults about my feminine behavior. I did feel like I understood the difference between boys and girls, however, although I knew I was a boy, in many ways I felt like a little girl inside and I found it very difficult to hide that fact in my outward behavior.

Over my many years of feeling different and being judged by others, I began to learn to expect the cruel name-calling. Much of my childhood was spent alone and crying, trying to make sense of it all. I often tried to defend myself verbally against others in an attempt to try to protect my innocence, but no matter how hard I tried, it did no good trying to persuade my opponents about my sexuality. While most children saw their childhood as a time of fun, excitement, and opportunity to explore the world, I spent much of my time just trying to exist in a world of fear, hurt, and pain. As a child I felt life was so unfair and I taught myself not to speak much because talking only brought more unwanted attention my way. For many years, I wanted no part of this cruel world.

I will never forget when I was about five years old; a teenaged neighbor invited my sister and me outdoors to play. This teenager suggested that my sister and I dig into his pants pocket to retrieve a quarter, which was impossible without rubbing his erection. After he got the attention he wanted, he noticed our facial expressions of disgust and laughed out loud before running away. I often try to make myself remember who this guy was and I guessed this was a joke he played on many of the neighborhood children, particularly the little girls. However, I certainly didn't find any humor in his sick joke. I can only guess that because so many people took me for such a different little boy it was supposed to be okay to play this kind of joke on me. I could not imagine that he invited all little boys to massage him in this way; another indication of how different other people saw me.

While attending middle school my classmates often made

fun of me because of being different. By now it was very clear that I was different from other children, little boys in particular. To be frank, I now understand that I had very effeminate ways although I truly tried to act as normal as possible. Acting "normal" was such a challenge for me because I didn't know how to act like other little boys. In fact, throughout my childhood no one took the time to show me or mentor me in the way I was supposed to grow. I was bright enough to understand that most people would rather make fun of those who were different rather than try to make a difference in their lives.

My early memories sometimes haunt me even now, as I often recall how as a young child I was not only molested by adult men, but how I also had to endure several sexual encounters with little boys in the neighborhood, boys who often made fun of me when they were around other neighborhood children. I will admit that the sexual encounters with little boys my age started mostly as playful childhood games. However, once these games advanced what I knew for sure was that the sexual activities which took place between several of the neighborhood boys and myself were more than just games, they were very real. The little boys involved certainly didn't show any signs of being different from me, which left me even more confused about my sexuality and the sexual activities that transpired between us. How could a child as young as me be exposed to such sexual acts when most kids were playing with Barbie dolls, baking cookies with their easy-bake-ovens, or concentrating on football and other various sports? It seemed that while they struggled with normal kid issues most of my days were being spent with me struggling with the fact that I had been exposed to sexual activities; homosexual ones at that.

My childhood sexual activities with other little boys and adult men turned out to be detrimental to me into my adulthood. As I matured I could see that many of the little boys who engaged in those mischievous sexual encounters with me finally got a grip on their sexuality by their young adult years. But for me, as I got older, I began to develop feelings for teenage boys that I could not explain. It was obvious that I was attracted to little boys, teenage boys, and adult men; to sum it up I was simply attracted to most everything concerning the same sex. In many ways, it was like I was attracted to the masculinity I lacked as a little boy. While many of the little boys that engaged in sexual activities with me as a child began to live normal lives and develop relationships with girls, I, on the other hand, could not explain my growing feelings for boys—feelings that caused me to continue to dislike myself in the same way that other people did.

Even as I matured kids and others never stopped calling me unpleasant names, which did not make matters in my life any better. The self-loathing I felt inside got even worse. For many years as a teenager I hid my feelings inside—feelings about how I felt towards other boys. Although most of the teasing came from boys, I still wanted a strong connection with them. My emotions were yearning to be with them but each one insisted on informing me that I was a homosexual—something they made very clear to me that they didn't want to be near. My existence was like an easily transmitted or deadly plague, but I honestly felt I would outgrow my feminine behavior and the homosexual desires I had toward boys. I desperately wanted to be ALL BOY! I can't explain it but I knew the feelings that I had were not normal. I wanted to talk to someone about being so different but I didn't know who I could talk to. So, I would just stay to myself and hide away from everyone around me in fear; fear of continually being ostracized.

It seems surreal to me now when I think about myself being just five years old and the molestations I endured at the hands of older boys in the neighborhood, men as old as my father, and even my own older brother. I can recall that when the molestation began as a child it felt good because I had never experienced any affection or love from anyone. In many ways it felt very sincere to be loved in this way by my abusers but once I reached the age of 14, I wanted the molestations to stop because I knew they were not right. By then I knew that little boys were supposed to be attracted to girls and not boys, however, I felt trapped to find that I was only attracted to other boys.

At the age of 15, I decided to tell my mother about what I was feeling and what my brother and others had done to me. Honestly, I felt pressured to tell my mom because my oldest brother threatened to tell her about a sexual advance I had made towards him one morning. I attribute my behavior to being caused by the molestations I had experienced in my early childhood. Early one morning I found myself weak from wanting the affection of any older male. You see, it was mostly during early morning hours that I was seduced as a child. Because of this, what became normal to me was to yearn for that same kind of affection during this time of day. So, on this particular morning I approached my oldest brother who refused to take part in my sexual advance. I felt embarrassed when he refused to participate and I felt confused since my older brother had initiated several sexual encounters with me previously. However, this time he threatened to tell my mother all that had been going on with me for those many years if I did not tell her myself. I can remember that day as if it was yesterday. I was tormented with the decision to tell my mother about all the molestations because it meant that I would have to expose my brother along with the others who had taken sexual advantage of me. Not to mention I was unsure of how she would receive the information. I wondered if she would believe me and accept it or would she blame me for the activities that took place. Dealing with homosexuality would be something very different from having to deal with my sisters being pregnant. It was a topic that most people in my community had not yet openly dealt with. I wonder today if my oldest brother had not threatened to tell my mother about my advance towards him and my other secrets, would I have ever told anyone about what I had been involved in? I loved my mother so much and I did not want to break her heart. I admired her commitment to being a good mother and providing for her six children. While most people seemed only to talk about the love they had for their mothers, my love was strong because I felt she already knew about me and had accepted how different I was as a child. That is not to say that when she felt I was acting like a girl my mother would not chastise me, because she often did. However, most of my behavior must have become normal to her because I was comfortable playing with my sisters' Barbie dolls and being a part of other girl activities in front of her.

While I never blamed my parents for being different, I did feel that many other people helped attribute to my feminine behaviors. I often sought protection from my parents but in many ways they really could not provide the safety I needed since most of the accusations and name-calling took place away from home. Although, when my siblings teased me by calling me ugly names, my parents would insist that they stop. However, the name-calling never really stopped and I just learned to understand this to mean that kids were going to be kids.

The day I informed my mother about my sexual encounters and molestations was one of the most challenging days of my youth. At this point in my life I wasn't as ashamed of being abused as much as I wanted to just change my behaviors. As a child I always felt that my mother could fix everything in my life because I believed mothers always had all the answers. So, as my mother entered the house from work, I approached her at the door. She could tell that something was wrong because I just stared at her with a look of hopelessness on my face. As I began to speak, my words seemed to come out like a riddle. I tried to explain to her about my feelings of homosexuality and about all the men who had taken advantage of me. I don't recall getting her full attention until I stated that my brother was one of my abusers. I recall her brushing the accusation off because perhaps she was so hurt inside that she didn't really know how to respond. I felt so bad that I just wanted to be embraced and held for a moment but instead my mom just suggested that I see a doctor for help. She began pacing the floor and picking up things avoiding eye contact with me. In a way I was really relieved that I had confessed to her and felt it was up to her to digest the information the best way she knew how. I refused her advice that I obtain a doctor's help because I knew there wasn't a pill in the world that could make my feelings go away. All I could do was think about all the things that took place up until that point in my childhood and hope one day to erase all the memories and pain that I thought were too much for any child to face. I wanted a normal childhood like other children had but I had no idea that my life had been forever changed.

WELCOME TO MY WORLD

I certainly had much resentment towards the world that I was now a part of because, not only had my innocence been stolen from me but I had been raped of my mental and emotional soundness as well. In many ways I would have rather been dead because somehow I knew I would never be able to fully recover my life. Although I was still alive by the time I reached adolescence, I felt so many pieces of the puzzle of my life were missing. I spent the entirety of my teens trying to make sense of it all. As a teen I often enjoyed observing people and from afar most people generally appeared to enjoy their lives. I would sit back in a corner watching other kids gather together outside to play games most children enjoyed playing. They seemed to have so much fun but I only watched wishing I could be a part of the excitement. There were rare times when I would try to be involved and play with the neighborhood kids. However, it was usual for the popular teens to hold leadership positions in the games, and at the beginning at each game these leaders had the power to select players for their team. While I wanted to be a part of a team, I never had the opportunity to be selected. I would gather with the rest of the crowd of youths, expressing an interest in being selected. While the last selections were being made, I would yell and scream at the top of my lungs begging to be picked for one of the teams. This was to no avail because no one had any trust or confidence in me. How could I expect them to when I certainly didn't exude any confidence in myself?

Even now when I recall telling my mother about my lifestyle, I can also recall the look on her face—her expression said it all. She really was concerned but not really alarmed, as if she had already known about my secret lifestyle. How could she deny my feminine behaviors and the constant name-calling? Like most mothers, she had to have had an intuition about those things that involved her children. However, I know she truly didn't have a clue about the details of what those individuals did to me nor the particulars of my involvement with my older brother. I remember how calm she remained after I told her about the many sexual encounters I endured with older men and with my own brother. I couldn't tell if she remained calm because of the embarrassment I had caused her and my family, or if it was that she felt responsible for my pain. Her first reply was that she would schedule an appointment for me to see a therapist and a doctor. It was almost as if she really believed she had said something to comfort me. In spite of what she felt were positive comments, the message I received was that she really didn't understand my battle. You did not have to be a rocket scientist to see that I wasn't a normal child. The issues of homosexuality were much too deep for her or anyone at that time to understand. We are talking about understanding homosexuality in the early 1970's.

When I declined therapy, my mother found herself as helpless as I had become, because she thought doctors would have had the cure I needed. Although I lived in a two-parent home, my parents had other issues which were much bigger than treating a son suffering from the plague of homosexuality. They were dealing with the slow economy and providing food and shelter for me and my five siblings. So, how did my mother deal with my plight and refusal to seek professional help? The

31

support my mother ultimately provided me with was LOVE. She showered me with unconditional LOVE.

After our conversation neither my mother nor I ever talked about my situation again to one another. I wondered if she had discussed our conversation with my father because he began serving me the same prescription my mom had prescribed; a lot of LOVE.

Homosexuality back then was not a popular issue and the subject was condemned by most people. Few embraced those who participated in this lifestyle. While my mom did continue to show love for me, I know she not only felt helpless but also felt embarrassed about my homosexuality. For me, life continued as normal as possible for a young teenager such as I had become. Of course, the teasing continued, and although I received unconditional LOVE from both my parents it didn't help my inner struggles or take away my symptoms of homosexuality. My outward shame was displayed on my face daily because I didn't know how to dig deep down inside of myself to accept or deal with who I was. I usually locked myself in my room, spending much time imagining what it would be like to be a whole person. Sometimes I would wonder if it were at all possible for me to embrace who I was, imagining what it would be like to have a real boyfriend. Still, although I was only a young teenager I often question myself on what I really knew about life.

Physically, I was petite and very light weight. I use the word petite because I was so tiny I could wear my sisters' clothes rather than my brothers'. When I was a young teen, Afros, corn-rolls, and plaits were very popular much like they are today. If my sisters didn't have time to braid or plait my hair, I usually did it myself. My pettiness, wearing braids in my hair, and my feminine behavior, only brought me more unwanted attention and more opportunities for name-calling. In many ways I had grown accustomed to the hate brought upon me from classmates, neighborhood kids and even adults, and my size didn't do much for me to help my insecurities. I looked so much like a girl, that boys would sometimes mistake me for being one and at high school dances they would mistakenly ask me to dance. During these times, I knew things had gone too far.

Such incidents during my teenage years made me feel even more insecure. I continued to spend much of my time confused about my life. As I began to make friends, the pattern became that I would befriend girls who found me to be a lot of fun. These friendships led to some positive relationships. Although I wished that I could desire to be more than friends with the females who befriended me, I learned to accept that I only desired them as friends. Usually, the girls that befriended me were not in the popular crowd and looked as hopeless as I did. This didn't bother me much because I just wanted someone I could talk to and spend time with. I will admit that these friendships were not on the same level as most friendships because I was not yet ready to go public with the fact that I was homosexual.

When we hung out, my girlfriends and I talked mostly about guys they thought were attractive. I don't know why but the same guys that most of my girlfriends found attractive, I did as well. Many times I wanted to say out loud that I agreed with the choices of boys they found attractive. My girlfriends sometimes would ask me what girls I found attractive and I always selected cheerleaders or majorettes because I not only thought they were the prettiest, but I also wanted to be one of them. In reality I knew that if I had been interested in girls in that way, hell would have frozen over before any of those particular girls found me attractive. Girls that were cheerleaders and majorettes were considered the elite of the school. They only dated popular guys on the football and basketball teams; those considered the most sought after guys in school. Popular girls certainly discriminated!

Sometimes my girlfriends would try to get me to comment

33

about guys who they thought might be gay but I always declined to respond. I usually brushed them off by laughing with them as if what they were saying was funny. However, I usually felt very empty inside after laughing, because I should have defended their accusations against the homosexual in question.

I thought that most teenagers seemed to have great self-esteem in many ways. But, I personally could not begin to have self-worth about the person I had become. I was too affected by the loneliness and the constant harassment of others. I wanted so much to be identified as a regular teen and I began showing signs of depressing by becoming withdrawn and feeling empty and worthless. I also began experiencing crying spells and lacked motivation.

It was virtually impossible to maintain a normal quality life like other teens had. Again, I became so frustrated with my life and began wondering what the purpose was for my existence. I so badly wanted a friend who could identify with my lifestyle or one who would accept me. I longed for acceptance, but I knew meeting someone who could identify with my struggle would not be easy. Yet, I would have settled for anyone I could call a trustworthy friend.

Establishing friendships with females did satisfy me in many ways, because females never seemed to be concerned with my sexuality or feminine ways. Instead they saw me as just another girlfriend. Although my girlfriends were the very least attractive girls in the neighborhood, I posed no real threat to them as other females did. As my friendships began to grow with several females, I began to start feeling a little better about myself. Some people seemed to oppose and be concerned about me having friendships with so many females, but this didn't make much sense to me because for many years no one wanted to be my friend at all. My mother, sisters, brothers, and others in the neighborhood didn't understand why I had to be around so many girls all the time. They couldn't make the connection between them and me. In other words, what could a girl and I have in common with each other? To the outsider I was a homosexual. I guess they thought that I had accepted the fact that I was a homosexual so much so that I now wanted to be a girl by surrounding myself around so many of them. Many of the neighborhood boys assumed that I was no longer a homosexual because they thought I had begun dating the many girls I was with. This was something they had begun to admire about me. No matter what anyone thought or why I wasn't really concerned, because I was just glad to have people around me who at least casually cared. I do think my parents were glad that I was beginning to open up a little more to people, which is something I had never done before. This wasn't such a bad thing to me either because I had always spent so many years alone. In many ways I was very excited that I was generating positive gossip throughout the community for a change—the "faggot" as they had called me, was now somewhat free, at least in theory.

FREEDOM

Even though I had become an introvert, I could now feel a change coming over my life and it felt wonderful! The shackles felt as if they were about to fall off of me, but I still wasn't completely free because I had the inner battle of homosexuality to deal with. However, because of my new friendships I no longer had to think about my inner struggle as much—my friends became my outlet. Even so, there were times when someone would push that button which caused me to remember my inner battles again. When they pushed that button by calling me a faggot or worse, then and only then would I think about that demon of homosexuality inside me. All in all, my self-confidence did begin to grow a bit because not only did I have friends, but I had friends who would defend me against anyone who disrespected me. By this time in my life I felt a growing sense of power. When people started to support me and rescue me, I began to feel as if I mattered.

My oldest sister Vanessa was my biggest supporter. She stood behind me no matter what anyone said about me. I can recall one of my first days at high school. Riding the bus home from school, a girl called me a faggot and my older sister said that she was going to beat her up when we got off the school bus. When the bus stopped and let us off, that particular girl and my sister began to fight. While the fight was going on the girl's sister jumped in the fight with a razor blade. I, in turn, jumped into the fight to stop the girl from hurting my sister and she sliced me across my face with the razor. Because of the intensity of the fight I didn't notice how badly I was cut. I was very lucky that day because the cut was very close to my jugular vein. To this day, people will ask me how I got the obvious scar on my face. If I was to be honest and tell them that I was cut because a girl called me a faggot it might start a conversation I don't want to get into, so I just tell them I cut myself shaving, which of course most people are too smart to really believe. I love when they say, "Chile, somebody tried to kill you." I think to myself, *Yeah, you're right—I got cut because some psychotic girl accused me of trying to steal her man.*

Many years later as an adult, I would still be very insecure because of low self-esteem and not knowing who or what I was. Can you imagine not having any self-esteem as a child, teenager, or even as an adult? The ridiculing I experienced had a hugely negative impact on me because I often found myself at a place where I thought no one would accept me as a person. I could not understand how a community would not have mercy on me as a child because of this infirmity I was struggling with. I often found myself crying and feeling so worthless and lonely. Yet, even through my loneliness I knew deep inside that I was very special. A sweet spirit would speak to me in those lonely times and assure me that I was a special child; even so, most times I just found it difficult to face life from day to day. I could not understand why I was dealing with this spirit of homosexuality, which had always proven to be lonely and a depressing spirit.

A person dealing with this spirit is not only suffering but lost as well. I often looked for support from my brothers, sisters, and other family members, to protect me from the outside world. Instead, they often called me the same names

TRACY J. SIPP

that outsiders called me and I became immune to the names when they came from my siblings. Sometimes I felt that I had warranted the name-calling because I wasn't strong enough and could not act like the other boys. I wanted to play sports very badly as a teenager but I could never make the team. It was so bad that I wasn't even allowed to be the ball boy. I remember how the boys would make much fun of me during tryouts for the junior high school football and basketball teams. I wanted to do whatever I could to be accepted and have the name-calling stop. It angered me to think I might have never been a victim of this lifestyle had I not been sexually molested. The question I often asked was who was the weaker, the faggot or those who preyed on little boys and innocent children causing them to experience things that made them into broken adults? I truly feel that we should be very careful what we label others.

My experiences as a child were very devastating, so much so that they had an impact on me even into adulthood. Even then I would battle within to build my self-esteem, and I lacked social skills and had panic attacks because I did not know how to express myself when in the company of others. I truly had become such an introvert, all of which caused me to also become a very judgmental person. I hurt so badly sometimes that even as I turned 40; I found it very difficult to have relationships with people, particularly African American men. When I'd find myself in their presence, I'd panic and begin sweating uncontrollably, because I am always reminded of the physical hurt many have caused me and the names I was called. When I was a child, I didn't feel I would ever measure up to their standards and expectations and sometimes as an adult I would have to force myself not to feel this way.

I don't want to imply that my childhood years were all bad. I did find comfort in some things and in high school God sent a blessing when he allowed Antoine the captain of the 1980 basketball team to become my friend. I attended Mainland Senior High School in Daytona Beach, Florida; this was the

38

same high school that NBA player Vince Carter attended. Antoine Davis a great basketball player admired me as a dancer and always talked about how talented he thought I was and how he thought I should be in the performing arts program. He also knew that I was very popular with some of the most attractive girls at school and throughout the community. All athletes wanted to be associated with these girls. Somehow the cheerleaders, pom-pom dancers, and other beautiful girls established wonderful relationships with me, and Antoine certainly wanted to get to know these girls. I always made sure that he had the first pick from among them. Antoine's family consisted of five brothers who all were very athletic, and a younger sister who was a cheerleader. His mother also admired me and she hired me to train his sister to become a better dancer and cheerleader. I will admit that his family found our friendship to be a bit odd because of our background and interests. Although his brothers never came out and made comments about me being gay, they would sometimes tease me by inquiring about what sports I played when they knew I really didn't play any. At first, I was not sure how to respond to their many humorous jokes because they would often ask me about various sports plays and positions. I pretended to agree with anything that sounded correct, as if I really understood the many sports languages that I didn't have a clue about. I was always tempted to just tell his brothers that I was a silent member of the high school cheerleading squad (as if they didn't already know). By Antoine being much older than his younger brothers I believed they trusted his judgment about our friendship and didn't dare tease him about being gay for hanging out with me. As time passed, our friendship grew and I became welcomed in Antoine's home. I became part of his family no matter how differently I acted or how his brothers actually saw me. From that point on, I never gave any thought to what his family thought of me because of my lack of athleticism. Most people at my high school thought Antoine was crazy by befriending me. I never talked about my sexuality with Antoine because people already talked about me too much, and I already assumed that he knew.

I had now been endorsed by one of our high school's most popular athletes. This was a major endorsement for me because it gave me the validation I dreamed of having as a person. We were not only friends, we became inseparable, talking on the telephone 2-3 times a day, every day. When the basketball team had to travel away on basketball tournaments, I felt lost because I had become so dependent on our friendship. Due to my insecurities, I often felt lonely and empty when he traveled away on tournaments. Sometimes, I even questioned our friendship, although he constantly reassured me by reminding me of how talented I was as a dancer. No matter how much attention Antoine received as a great athlete, he never let a day go by without reminding me that my talent as a dancer was just as equal to his athletic abilities. However, most people viewed our talents very differently which did make me feel like less of a person. Antoine also reminded me that he was proud to be my best friend because of the special gift God had given me as a dancer. When he spoke these kinds of words to me I felt like I could conquer the world. Being assured of my friendship with him somehow gave me the confidence I so desperately needed. He was so very special to me because I had love for him much different from the lustful love I felt for other males. It was genuine brotherly love. I wished others saw me as a real human being in the way that Antoine did, rather than some strange or freaky person. I'd always ask myself: why was it so difficult for people to see me as a normal kid?

When Antoine was away on basketball tournaments I would call his home over and over requesting to speak with him, only to be told by his family, "Tracy, he's still not back yet." Often, I would disguise my voice but his family would always recognize it was me and say, "He's still not back." I recall Antoine and I would talk until 3:00 a.m., either on the telephone or on one of the neighborhood corners, forgetting that we had to attend school shortly thereafter. I was obsessed with his friendship. Wherever he was, so was I especially after the basketball games. With his friendship I felt empowered and privileged. Most people had to accept me since they also wanted to be Antoine's friend. His female fan club was so huge that I was in charge of selecting which girls he dated or spent idle time with. After each basketball game you could expect his name to be front-lined in the local newspapers, which made his popularity grow even larger. Mainland Senior High School was integrated and very large; beautiful girls of all colors wanted to date Antoine.

At the end of my senior year, Antoine had made such a name for himself as a star basketball player that he was inducted into the 1980 Mainland Senior High School Hall of Fame, which led to a successful college basketball scholarship out of state. The ending of our close friendship changed my life because many of my insecurities were covered up by my friendship with him. After graduation Antoine chose to attend Marshall University, a prominent college in West Virginia which was over a thousand miles away. This change made the possibility of us continuing our friendship very challenging. Although we vowed not to let anyone take the other's place, I went back to being the insecure person afraid to face the world and although I found it hard to be in the world, God was with me. I prepared myself for my own college journey which I would find to be an impossible transition to make.

THE IDEAL ROLE MODEL

I recall the time when I was approximately ten years old; I met a much older teenager who was rumored to be a homosexual and a transsexual. Paige enjoyed cross-dressing as a female late at night, although I wasn't sure if he wanted to be a female or just enjoyed expressing himself by wearing female clothes. Everyone in my neighborhood knew and talked about him being a homosexual who had taken it to another level. The cross-dressing made him very different which of course caused people to whisper whenever he appeared in public, although most people kept their comments to themselves. I enjoyed seeing Paige and wanted to spend time with him because I felt he could explain how he was able to command the respect he received from the same kids that teased me. He appeared to be so comfortable with both his homosexual and transsexual lifestyles. Although it was against the norm in the 1970's to be open about one's homosexuality, Paige lived it with much confidence. As difficult as it must have been for them, his family did not condemn his behavior to the point where it damaged his self-esteem. His mother and father never chastised him about his homosexual lifestyle nor did they allow his brothers and sisters to make jokes about him in the way most siblings did. Paige had so much support from his parents that they allowed him to withdraw from high school so that he would not have to suffer the high school peer pressures that most children experienced. It was remarkable the way they supported and protected him from any backlash or ridicule he may have received from the community.

Although peer pressure was at an all-time high, Paige never allowed the opinions and negative comments of others to cause him to feel bad about himself nor strip him of his self-esteem. It was as if he were encouraged by the gossip directed at him and he continued living his life as he believed. I don't ever remember seeing Paige depressed during his early teenage years. I looked forward to the midnight hours, as a child, getting out of my bed to peek out of my bedroom window. This was the time that Paige would leave out of his home fully dressed as a woman. He often told me of how he would walk down Campbell Street, the main stretch of highway, where all the night clubs were. Here, he said was where he prostituted himself to heterosexual men. Although he did receive compensation, Paige expressed more enjoyment from the attention he got from men who enjoyed his favors. It didn't take long for the gossip to travel throughout the neighborhood about Paige's nightly female impersonations and the prostitution he participated in. However, he never showed any remorse or guilt. In fact, Paige seemed to show much pride in the way he could seduce and trick straight men; the very same ones who called him names during the day.

I admired Paige's strength and always wished that I could go with him at night to watch him perform. Paige was not a passive or introverted homosexual like many homosexuals become due to the embarrassment they face at the hands of others. He definitely didn't feel the shame I felt as a child which made him a role model for me, especially since I didn't find much joy in my own homosexual behaviors.

As a child in 1970, I didn't understand how any homosexual could appear to be so happy with the challenges of a lifestyle most people didn't understand or agree with. Paige certainly seemed to rise above the unpleasant names that most people called him; names like queer and freak. He just seemed to relish in the obvious hypocrisy of knowing that he was providing sexual favors by night to the very men and boys who called him names by day. Paige rarely cared about what females said about him because he saw females as his enemy and competition rather than potential friends. Some females tried to befriend him, confiding in him in the same way they confided in their girlfriends about being abused by their boyfriends and husbands. These were the same boyfriends and husbands that Paige picked up in the late hours of the night.

The image of the transsexual has changed dramatically since the 1970's. When guys dressed up as females in the 70's it was obvious to many that they were guys dressed up trying to look like girls, or simply freaks wanting attention. However, today with the help of cosmetic surgery, advances in hormone therapy, great makeup like MAC which is much thicker and more concealing, and other such tricks, transsexuals are able to achieve a softer look which gives them the upper hand at convincing others they are truly female.

So, Paige became my role model, simply because he was the only person who truly befriended the real me. I didn't want to be a girl or act like one, but I found comfort in being with him. He would talk with me about the homosexual lifestyle I was so afraid of living. I really wanted someone to understand or help me through this time in my life and protect me from all the hatred I was experiencing. Because the world hated those like me, I had become such a bitter individual and wanted to pay back hurt to all those who had caused me so much pain. If you are black, it is easy to identify with pain caused by ignorance and what we must understand is that ignorance breeds fear, and finally violence. When a person feels like they are up against a wall they will usually choose to fight back, and when this happens many innocent people get hurt!

I grew up angry and ultimately I did begin to seek out the type of love I was forced to learn as a child. The molestations I experienced as a little boy confused me into feeling it was a sort of love. I remember that it made me feel as if I had comfort and protection, at least it did from the prospective of a child. The strength and warmth I received from any strong black male created mixed feelings. I often felt powerless, helpless, weak, and yet loved, all at the same time. I never will forget what these feelings felt like. After being a part of a sexual experience with any male, including my brother, I began to trust them, and I often felt guarded and protected from the rest of the world. I looked forward to seeing them in the early mornings and late nights when it was time to be seduced. However, these same individuals that I felt protected by ran away from me when I'd see them in public, treating me as if I didn't exist. As a child I didn't know what to think about this behavior, and I always chose to think they had left suddenly for some important reason. When we were alone, these same guys were always nice to me and it wasn't until I got older that I understood why I was subjected to their mixed signals. I learned that some men were as confused as I was about their behaviors and sexuality.

What I thought was comfort as a child only turned out to be a nightmare when I became an adult living a full homosexual lifestyle. Needless to say, because of the many sexual encounters I experienced as a child I grew to become a very sexually active and promiscuous individual searching for love in all the wrong people. I often thought that my encounters with men, almost as old as my father, were secure because these older men always appeared to be strong like father figures. My own father provided well for me but he was unable to offer me real understanding, because at the time when I grew up most African American men felt their job was to provide food and shelter for their children. This was "doing their part" as a father. I appreciated having my father as a constant in my family because some children in my neighborhood didn't have fathers who were a part of their upbringing, but I wanted the kind of attention most children expected to receive from their fathers. In many ways this explained why my loneliness caused me to reach out to men who showed the slightest attention to me, no matter how inappropriate that attention was. Although I tried to hide the pain I felt inside, most people including my family thought I enjoyed being alone.

The men who raped and molested me used my pain to their advantage by preying on my innocence. For many years I enjoyed the attention they showed me and I don't ever recall being threatened by these men not to tell anyone about our secret acts. This was like an unspoken agreement between them and me. As a matter of fact, I don't recall them ever saying anything to me at all after the molestations. I was just happy to get the attention and they were happy to get what they wanted. At the time, I didn't realize how harmful and unacceptable this arrangement was.

WHO STOLE MY SOUL?

As a child, I spent much of my days and nights wondering how God could create a world with such lack of love and compassion. I wondered had anyone ever considered the fact that I was just a child who was struggling in a world I knew nothing about. I often wondered was this God the same God who spoke to me daily, helping to ease the pain that was inflicted on me by so many. I always felt like there had to be two separate Gods; the God who loved me and the God who protected those who persecuted me. As I got older, I understood that homosexuality was not right and the world I lived in was going to constantly remind me that I was not wanted. I also felt inside my heart that the God that loved me wanted me to change my lifestyle. The question was: "How do I make this change?" Perhaps I could make a change by trusting in my dreams.

My lifelong dream was to become a professional dancer and attend the Alvin Ailey Dance Academy in New York City. However, I knew I didn't have a chance at this because I did not have that special support needed from my parents and family to accomplish my dream. I also always dreamed of being on Broadway in *The Chorus Line* or *Dream Girls* (which featured Jennifer Holiday), but I knew there was no way to accomplish this either.

At the age of 17, I graduated from high school and was accepted to Florida State University. My acceptance at the university had its conditions because my high school grades were below average, which meant that I had to attend summer school prior to the fall semester to bring up my grades. While growing up, my grades always suffered because I was unable to focus due to the constant harassment I had to endure. After conditionally being accepted at Florida State University, I had no idea of what would be in store for me. When I arrived at the enormous campus, of one of the state's largest universities, I began to panic because I had never traveled away from home alone before. I questioned whether I could survive alone on my own. The large number of student enrollments overwhelmed me. The university was so large it felt like a major city or community and I just didn't realize the pressure I would be under trying to fit into this new environment where I did not know anyone. Also, remember, making friends had always been difficult for me so I didn't know how to begin making new friends at this larger than life university. I lacked social skills, and I had the mindset that if people didn't befriend me back home why would they befriend me at this university? I would panic when I had to leave my dormitory room in fear of being discovered. I wanted to pursue a degree in dance at Florida State University, a major that consisted of mostly white female students, yet, I also wanted to hide myself and not be discovered as a homosexual. Of course as it had always been, my secret was soon revealed, and my fear immediately kicked in.

I cried day and night in my dormitory room afraid to go to class because of people laughing and making fun of me. I simply felt that I had set myself up to fail. Feeling this was my reality. One day, I made a telephone call home and begged my parents to let me withdraw from the university and return home. They agreed and had my sister, who was attending

Florida A&M (FAMU) a nearby historical black university, pick me up and drive me to the Greyhound Bus Station.

While traveling home I felt little comfort. As I reviewed things over and over in my mind, I noticed an older black man on the bus trying to make eye contact with me. I was sitting in a seat on the opposite side of the bus and I could see him out of my peripheral vision trying to get my attention by stroking the outside of his private area. I found his behavior to be weird because I didn't know what had prompted his actions so I tried to ignore him, but he noticed my shyness and found a way to get my full attention by doing the unthinkable—he unzipped his pants and pulled out his fully erect penis. This was meant to show me that he was interested in me. Although there were a few other passengers on the bus, it was obvious that this stranger had only my attention. I had to ask myself if I had given him a sign that I wanted him in a sexual way or was he just a freak like the other men in my life that had molested me for their own gain. This terrified and excited me at the same time because I didn't know that these kinds of things could take place in cities other than my hometown.

I had learned early on that a perverted man in heat would have sex with anything as long as it satisfied his desires. Many would question how a grown man could have sex with a five-year-old boy. On the bus I began to wonder if all teenage boys got this kind of attention when they were away from home. I immediately thought the stranger who had got my full attention loved me, because after all this was exactly how all the other men in my life had shown me love and attention. This was truly a moment in my life I would never forget.

This risky behavior showed great boldness and desperation just to obtain an orgasm but it didn't surprise me coming from a man. After this encounter I became very inquisitive, wanting to learn more about the homosexual lifestyle. I often wondered why so many people opposed the homosexual lifestyle because it certainly felt right. After all, how was I supposed to know any differently because I had never had a normal sexual encounter with a female nor did I desire to.

A New Day

After returning back home from Florida State University, I enrolled in a community college to pursue an A.A. Degree in Communications with a Minor in Theater and Dance. I was 17 years old attending college in Daytona Beach and I found that I didn't have to endure as much verbal abuse now, as I had when I was a child. As a college student, people rarely called me names to my face; they now only talked about me behind my back and whispered negative comments to others. Of course, I thought this change in behavior would take some of the focus off me being a homosexual and help others see me as a normal human being. I now wanted to become my own person and I enjoyed wearing flamboyant clothes. Because I was a male student, my style was very different from that of my college peers and those who knew me in high school. Although most of the college students were from various cities around Florida, I felt as if I had an opportunity to impress students who had not yet formed an opinion about my homosexual lifestyle. What I learned as a homosexual was that I enjoyed dressing well and wearing the finest clothes, wanting to appear very neat to others. This was certainly a way of getting noticed. Because of the flamboyant clothes I wore it made me even more noticeable as a homosexual. Most guys

TRACY J. SIPP

wore very basic clothes to class but fashion would now become part of my new college life and personality. Of course, I received an overwhelming amount of attention from girls and guys which was not bad press in many ways, but it did bring me much unwanted attention from admirers of both genders. Because of my shyness I didn't know how to deal with the attention I was now receiving and it appeared to many of my new admirers as if I was arrogant. However, in many ways my flamboyant dressing helped me to hide and cover up my social disorder and the low self-esteem of a homosexual. I usually went to class and then went directly home, not interacting with the other students because of my low self-esteem. It helped that I lived at home away from the students who lived on or near campus. I wanted desperately to befriend the many admirers but I could not break the shell that years of abuse had caused me. As I tried to change, I would often panic and breakout into uncontrollable sweats. The switch in college majors from dancer to communications major was clearly my way of helping others see me as more than a homosexual wanting to become a dancer. I wanted to be seen as a normal college student.

I knew I'd never realize my real dream of attending the Alvin Ailey Dance Academy, but it certainly did not stop me from dreaming. I was not only dealing with the reality that I was not going to attend the prestigious academy, but I was also preparing myself for the adventure of what I thought would be a lifetime. While attending college closer to home, I learned that my lifestyle was only going to get more challenging and confusing. I had now crossed over to becoming an adult and although inside I wrestled with the feelings of a homosexual I was not yet willing to surrender my soul to the lifestyle. I still had hopes and dreams of living a normal life by finding the desire to marry a beautiful woman and have children. I could be proud of that kind of life even if I had to fake it. While I did eventually seek out relationships with females, hoping that my

52

feelings towards them would change into something lasting, for me the struggle of homosexuality was so strong that I could not ignore the attraction I felt toward those of the same sex. In the presence of a special man, my hormones would race through my body causing my emotions to run wild. The blood in my veins would also begin rushing to the most intimate part of my body causing me to lose control in the area most noticeable for a male. For many homosexuals this was their same struggle but trying to explain this to heterosexuals only made us sound weird, freaky, and very sexually abnormal. Losing control of my body was weird even to me because I didn't understand what was causing me to react with such passion toward other men. It felt like my body was being possessed with something I couldn't explain, and I despised the times when I had to come in contact with an attractive guy. No matter how well I controlled my thoughts, I guess I didn't know how closely connected my mind and body were. Yet, in my mind I was still convinced that I could change the inability to control myself when I was near men, even with the fact that I had been sexually abused as a child.

For so long I felt I had spent so much time trying to prove things to myself and others that I finally decided to begin living. I started making my own decisions and I tried not to care about what others thought about my lifestyle. I had spent enough time in my life trying to please those who obviously didn't give a damn about me, and I learned that when people didn't agree with how different you were they often criticized but rarely offered helpful solutions. It was clear that at this point in my life, as a young adult, I would not be able to convince people that I wanted to be heterosexual and not homosexual. I would never be able to convince people of how badly I had been used, and how it had adversely affected my life up to that point.

I had attempted relationships with two older men around this time, and learned after the fact that one was a distant cousin and the other was his very close friend. Again, both guys were very smart, handsome, and in good standing in my community. There were rumors about them both being homosexual but they acted very masculine and showed no signs of being in the lifestyle. Most importantly, both of them had very impressive careers and I looked up to them wanting so much to be like them. I don't know what they both saw in me because I felt like such a nobody but during my first two years back home after my Florida State crisis, I became sexually involved with both men. Neither knew about the other (or so I thought), although when I think about it now I believe they could have set me up because my experience tells me that men will be men; especially in this lifestyle.

Conquering the Drag Dream

While at home my other passion was spending as much time with my baby sister as possible; helping to prepare her for the world. I used to help her as a way to avoid the real issues I was dealing with. I lived through my sister who had become an icon to so many people back home. Many thought she was the perfect "All-American" black girl. She was the black girl next door. Since my dreams of becoming a dancer and choreography quickly faded I began to live my dreams through the life of my baby sister. She loved the attention, stage, and spotlights, which came with performing. I gave up my dream of becoming a dancer to begin coaching and preparing her for pageants and dance competitions. I didn't mind giving up my dream because I felt that as long as they saw her they would have to notice me. I masterminded this plan so people would no longer just see me as a homosexual but as a gifted and talented individual. Whenever I learned of a big competition coming to the Florida area, I would immediately begin to prepare my sister without asking for her input. During this time racial barriers were still a difficult thing in Daytona Beach, Florida, but to me that didn't matter because I knew I had the ability to make her a winner which would keep the spotlight on me as well.

I will never forget her first competition in 1978. My sister was a cheerleader in middle school just like most little girls. To be a cheerleader was one of the biggest dreams a black girl could aspire to at the time because it was difficult for any black person to see themselves as being successful. My sister, I will admit, was a very beautiful dark-complexioned girl who often got overshadowed by girls with lighter skin. Yet, she had a way of shining through; much like Diana Ross did back in her heyday. In fact, I did tend to compare her to Diana Ross because like Diana she may not have been the most beautiful young lady in the world, but she could win over her audience with her charisma. This was the key to being an entertainer. Most people lacked this natural ability because they thought if they could sing or dance it would be enough to succeed in the world of entertainment. However, I always knew that it didn't always take great talent to be a great star. For many, great performing was the key for success. This way of training my sister to think led to her to become a huge success.

At any rate, I decided to enter my baby sister into the Miss Campbell Junior High School Pageant. This was a competition that white girls usually won. Pageants in general consisted primarily of white girls, because black girls had not yet come to understand the purpose behind parading around in beautiful gowns. Black girls at that time also did not understand that these kinds of competitions helped build self-esteem and opened doors to successful entertainment careers. White girls understood that the pageant was one way to fame and fortune, which often led to modeling and acting careers. While the average black girl was still focusing on making the cheerleading squad I knew that I had to move my sister to the next level of competition.

When I entered my sister into the Miss Campbell Pageant it didn't matter to me if she won or lost because I saw this event as just the beginning of the prepping stage for both of us. I had never coached a pageant contestant before and she had never entered one, however, the little black girl next door was about to get noticed and so was I. I had strategically figured out how we would bring this whole thing together, because financially my parents didn't have the kind of money needed to purchase the gowns white girls won in. Nor were my parents interested in having her be a part of this level of competition. I had a plan in mind that was sure to work. So, I began coaching her on how to walk, sit, and speak, for pageant interviews. I taught her choreographed routines and showed her how to be a stage performer in ways that would command the audience's attention. The real competition was modeling evening gowns so I decided to have my sister ask her white girlfriends to borrow their prom and homecoming gowns. They were glad to help her.

When my baby sister began competing in the big league, I often worried about the swimsuit competition; an area she suffered in because like most black girls, she had weight issues. Mainstream pageant judges usually equated beauty with being thin. This explained why in the late 1970's, "Miss Black" pageants became very popular. The black community started their own pageants, because they knew we could not be judged on physical beauty in the same way that white girls could. Although I didn't believe that black girls got fair judging in mainstream pageants, I didn't value black pageants the same. Starting "Miss Black" pageants, in my opinion, was agreeing that black girls didn't have what it took to compete with white girls. I knew that black girls were just as gifted to compete, as long as they committed themselves to the challenge.

My sister entered that first pageant and the rest was history. Her crowning ceremonies began. She went from middle school queen to local and state competitions; all the way to the Miss Florida competition. The state of Florida was in an uproar because the little black girl next door was upsetting the state norm. She was headlined in the front pages of local newspapers. Now, keep in mind that my sister was competing against the finest white girls around and taking home the prizes

TRACY J. SIPP

and crowns. Everyone began to take notice of her winnings and of course I was in the mix as her coach and the mastermind behind the prominent queen.

After several years of this, my fantasies came to an end. She was no longer a little girl and would be leaving me to attend college. My baby sister could have easily attended almost any college or university she chose to but, I felt she would benefit most from attending a historical black college. With her experience as a cheerleader, dancer, and performer, I saw her becoming a cheerleader for one of the top NFL teams like the Dallas Cowboys. Convincing her to put her college education on hold to become a professional cheerleader was not an option. Robin, who had always entrusted me with every major decision for her life, had dreams of her own. She appreciated me for the life I had helped give her through pageants, national dance competitions, and other arenas, but as exciting as these things were she ultimately wanted to be a career woman and I certainly had to agree. I didn't think being a career woman was such a bad idea because I thought she'd still have a chance to become a news anchor in a major city; a position that definitely had its celebrity benefits. So, I immediately began the search for which college would be best for her to attend.

While attending my older sister's football homecoming game at FAMU in Tallahassee, Florida, I had the awesome privilege of attending the homecoming parade that featured the Tuskegee, Alabama marching band. Historical black colleges have always been known for their band performances and the excitement of the battling of their bands. Although black colleges did also have great athletes, they often suffered because of budget constraints. College bands played a major role in drawing people into football games. When I saw the Tuskegee marching band, I knew that this was the college for Robin. While it is true that every black college band had a way of bringing excitement through their dazzling performances, when I saw the Tuskegee band and the marching Piperettes (the girls who marched with the band), I was reminded of the New York City Rockettes; only these black girls were a high stepping, high kicking, dance college group. I could not believe their beauty and the jazzy costumes they wore. My eyes were glued to the dancing Piperettes as I walked side by side with them, following them to the end of the parade. I became so excited with their performance that I returned home to Daytona Beach to let Robin know about this great marching band.

Robin was not just my sister, she had become my best friend, my confidant, and my, in a sense, trophy, who I still wanted to showcase to the world. Although she still didn't know the secret life I was living and the shame and guilt I carried every day, I felt she would not judge me. It appeared that girls loved me because I had the ability to bring the best out of them and get them noticed. I had so many requests from parents in my community to coach their daughters for pageants and dance competitions, but it wasn't until now at age 40 that I've come to understand their requests were an honor back then. I really wasn't interested in working with other girls although people in the neighborhood always referred to me as being the one who worked well with girls. As long as I was coaching and teaching girls, the perception was that I was no longer a "faggot."

I remember a wonderful disco singer by the name of Gloria Gaynor. She recorded a great song entitled "I Will Survive." The lyrics were a perfect anthem for me, and I held on to them even until this day. Because of that song, I ultimately learned to walk with my head up high a little higher and I tell the devil to go to hell because he wasn't welcome near me. I learned to roll my eyes at harassers and walk with my head up high when people made fun of me; this was all a part of my struggling desire to acquire self-esteem.

Girls felt they needed me in order to win and they continued to try to hire me to help them with local and state competitions. Neighborhood boys saw me as the tool to help them get dates with the most popular and attractive girls in the community. I learned that being a gifted homosexual had its advantages.

Courage

I've learned that most people appear to have it all together but in reality they are just as weak as I often felt. They just hide their hurt behind hurting others. Of course, I realized early that words had so much power. Parents taught their children to say "Sticks and stones may break my bones but words will never hurt me." This showed that parents were just as ignorant as their children, because words are very powerful. Sticks and stones may break the bones but words can very often break the spirit.

In 1982, I was preparing to graduate from the Daytona Beach community college with my associate degree in communications and I thought it was time for me to leave the small town of my childhood. I felt ready to experience life in a big city or at least in a city bigger than the one I had been raised in. Although my dream of becoming a Broadway dancer had ended many years before and my attempt to attend college away from home had failed the first time, I felt it was high time for me to step outside my comfort zone. I didn't know if I was totally ready to face the bigger world but I somehow knew that there was no better time to make a move. I thought my past hurts would be forgotten if I left the place where I sustained my injuries. By the time I was ready to leave Daytona Beach, I found it hard to believe that I had found some acceptance from local residents. Even in high school I had been voted most likely to succeed.

Now, I was certainly in search of whom I was and Daytona Beach could not offer the answers I sought. I felt I wanted to move where the homosexual lifestyle was more acceptable (which I came to understand was virtually nowhere). I desperately needed someone to help me find myself in this world, and I thought that only homosexuals who could find peace with themselves were those who befriended other homosexuals. Everyone else seemed to be failing us. Black churches avoided addressing homosexual issues, other than preaching that all homosexuals were going to hell. Church members seemed to often enjoy hearing preachers tell the homosexual to change their behavior or go to hell. They often paraphrased, "God made Adam and Eve and not Adam and Steve." How many times did homosexuals have to continue to hear that overused slogan being preached by virtually every preacher behind the church pulpit? As if using that slogan had real power to make homosexuals change their sinful behavior. They fail to understand that being a homosexual is not like being an alcoholic. It is more like a defect or imbalance in the human makeup; a brain imbalance has always been my theory and explanation for homosexuality. Whatever the cause, our struggle continues due to lack of real research. I feel if scientists can discover a pill to help cure depression in millions of people then they certainly can find a way to assist with the imbalance of the homosexual. How else could one explain the cause of homosexual behavior? As I continued to pray to God about my spirit of homosexuality, I considered that it might only be a phase in my life, even though I am aware that I have had these feelings since I was a child of five years old. When I see children at that age, I can't help but think about how some parents try to protect them from this spirit by not allowing homosexuals around them as if it could rub off. I have heard

THE CRY OF A LITTLE BOY

that if a child was molested then he would become a molester himself, however, I've always known in my heart that I could never inflict on another child the pain that was inflicted on me. The thought of ruining a child's life and leaving them with so much guilt and shame is something I could never do.

In the early 1980's there was a movement that took place within the homosexuality community and I wanted to be near it. I thought if I could be where other homosexuals were then I could find out more about myself. I just wanted someone to create a dialogue in order to find out if there was treatment for this spirit which was taking over my life. I knew there were others like me, wanting to feel a part of the movement, who also wanted a purpose in their life that could not be found anywhere else. The years of isolation were weighing heavy on me, and as they say, if you can't beat 'em, why not join them? With all of the negative experiences I had gone through so far in my life, I just needed to make sense of them and find some worth. I didn't know where this journey would lead me but I decided to let the journey begin. I continued to pray every day hoping that God would not forsake me; praying that he would not punish me before I gained some understanding of the life I had been dealt. During the winter semester of 1983, I enrolled in Morehouse College in Atlanta, Georgia. When I arrived in Atlanta, I was overtaken by a complete culture shock. First of all, Morehouse College has an all-male student body and all I saw were hundreds of African American men; more young men than I had ever seen at one time. It didn't have the feel of a college but more like a large male fraternity. I was in disbelief at all the beautiful black men of every shade and size on campus. There were light, dark, short, tall, small, medium, and large built black men. I thought being there was everything I had dreamed of and I must admit I also felt a real sense of accomplishment at being accepted to this very historical and prominent black college that many young men only dreamed of attending.

Although I had heard rumors about Morehouse College having gays in attendance, I immediately dismissed the rumors, chalking them up as being spread by those who only wanted to discredit this wonderful institution. I felt honored that there was a college that recognized young African American men, proving that all young black men were not aspiring to be convicts. I was only 19 years old when I arrived at Morehouse College, and I soon realized that even the abuses I received in Daytona Beach had not prepared me for what I would personally face at Morehouse. The majority of men at Morehouse were not gay and it became clear that you would easily get beat down if you were gay and didn't stay in your place. I began to feel the eyes of everyone looking at me and I would panic because I knew these young men would be able to tell that I was not a normal guy. I began to live in fear and never left my dormitory room for fear of facing criticism. In the dormitory building I lived in I met a couple of guys from Miami, which made me feel a little comfort because they were from my home state. But, my assigned roommate was from the Virgin Islands and he hated me. Because I had not known how to make friends, particularly with men, I felt it best to stay secluded in my room. This did not sit well with my roommate who enjoyed having his girlfriend (a Spelman College student) over. He was not the most outgoing person either, and it seemed that having a relationship with her was his way of handling it. He began to resent me for staying in our room so much and this started a real war between us. There were rumors around campus that my roommate was bi-sexual but I found it hard to believe because he seemed to be quite content with the relationship he had with his girlfriend. It would be years later that I'd learn these rumors were true. All I know is that after a couple of months of living with this guy, it became obvious to me that he did seem very different from the other heterosexual guys but I just couldn't put my finger on exactly why. I will admit he was a very quiet person who rarely said anything. The vibes we both gave off to each other made it very uneasy in our living quarters, especially since I would often walk in on him and his girlfriend during their most intimate moments. In an attempt to give him the room I would reach out to my newfound friends in the city and try to spend as much time as possible with them, but this caused me to neglect my studies. It got to the point where the only time I would return to my room was to get a change of clothes. Because of the fear and shame of being around other men, I refused to take showers in the dormitory, knowing this was a place where hundreds of men gathered every morning and it terrified me to gather with other men in a shower room. I felt this would fully expose me and I couldn't handle the pressure of trying to hide my feelings. I knew I would be easily physically aroused at seeing other naked men, which was something I had always hated about being a male; not being able to hide becoming excited. I remember the first time I encouraged myself to go to the shower room, I noticed a janitor much older than the other students, walking around the shower stalls looking at them taking showers. I don't think any of the other guys noticed him because it was so early in the morning and most of the guys were still pretty sleepy, but I immediately took notice of this fatherly looking man because he resembled many of the men that had seduced me when I was a child. The man was fully clothed and I began to look him up and down when I noticed that he had an erection. His erection did not seem normal because it was larger than anything I had witnessed before. This certainly alarmed me because Morehouse was an excellent institution of higher learning and I could not believe that men like him were hired and represented the college. I was in fear that the other guys would notice him, so I gathered my personal belongings and ran back to my room without showering. I knew it would be a long rocky road for the next couple of years (if I would make it).

THE MADNESS BEGINS

I began to spend more and more time away from the campus and with my newfound friends who were mostly young African American homosexuals experimenting and learning about their sexuality. Many of these guys felt relieved to know there were so many other homosexuals in Atlanta, because this gave them validation and self-worth. There were many like me struggling with the spirit of homosexuality. This is about the time when I began having sexual encounters with guys my own age. Being with them was not that different from the sexual encounters I experienced with much older men as a child, and I was just happy about finally being able to acknowledge what I had always tried to hide.

My grades began to suffer greatly because I was spending too much time with my friends, but still at the time I had no regrets. The new homosexual movement was definitely on the rise especially in the city of Atlanta, and I soon realized that I had to make a very important decision about my education at Morehouse. I didn't know how I was going to get out of school because I had already convinced my parents to allow me to quit Florida State University. I knew I could not use the same excuse, but I did feel intimidated at having so many guys around me on campus. How was I supposed to focus on my education when I was so busy thinking about how afraid I was of being harassed about my sexuality? So, I took my focus completely off my education at Morehouse, and started focusing on finding people in the city of Atlanta who were more like me.

While I was deciding how to tell my parents that I wanted to leave Morehouse, I did try to find some enjoyment in the campus environment. I enrolled and enjoyed dance classes at Spelman College mainly because I was befriended by a very popular young lady who later went on to win the prestigious title of Miss Maroon & White (Miss Morehouse). This was a dream every girl on campus had, and because of my background in pageant coaching and dance, Miss Maroon & White and I became good friends. It was good to see that I still had the gift that could help girls become winners and help them shine. This helped me to realize just how badly I wanted to be a dancer and that I had definitely enrolled in the wrong college.

Preparing my friend Debbie, Miss Morehouse, for the first ever Miss Black Collegiate Pageant was a true test. My baby sister who was now attending Tuskegee University was also prepping for the Miss Tuskegee Pageant. She would not qualify to compete for the upcoming Miss Black Collegiate Pageant because she wasn't expected to reign as queen until the following year. However, to our surprise my sister not only won the Miss Tuskegee Pageant the following year, but the current winner had forfeited the opportunity to travel to Miami, Florida, to compete in the upcoming collegiate pageant. This indeed was a Godsend because this would give me an opportunity to see if I still had it. I was surprised and torn between coaching Debbie and my sister, Miss Tuskegee University. Feeling obligated to coach my sister I still felt a sense of loyalty to Miss Morehouse because of the support she had offered me while in school at Morehouse. However, my sister had always depended on me when it came to competitions, so I encouraged her not to worry about the upcoming competition and I prepared to help her with less than one week's notice.

To be fair, I began to coach Debbie for the 75 Plus Black Colleges and Universities Collegiate Competition. When the competition ended in Miami, Florida, Miss Morehouse was crowned as the first Miss Collegiate winner. This was a really big deal for me because it allowed me to shine much brighter. However, truthfully the gratification for me was not nearly the same as when my sister had won competitions because unlike Debbie, my sister made sure that I received a lot of the credit that came from her winnings. Debbie wasn't about to allow me to share her spotlight at all.

I do recall Debbie asking me about my sexuality and suggesting that I seek help so I might open up and tell my sister my secret. At this time I was still in denial but I did appreciate Debbie's compassion and advice. The question for me was even if I revealed it, who would be able to help me overcome my struggle with my homosexuality? By this time in my life I knew that people often said one thing and felt another in their hearts. Like church folk, they often talked about having compassion but only for certain sins. They would seek out how they could help people who were hurting, but those people didn't include the homosexual because most people felt the spirit of homosexuality was something most men chose to partake in. This is clearly a true sign of ignorance. At any rate, my new environment did help me discover that there were guys who were gay and didn't mind letting anyone know. But, I had learned to be very judgmental even of them because of my childhood. Because I had no self-esteem due to the embarrassment of being gay, I immediately learned to judge those who were openly gay. The people who harassed me as a child had convinced me that all homosexuals were the same. In other words, if you demonstrated any homosexual traits you were automatically looked upon as being one. In my life I learned that when I judged other homosexuals, it only helped perpetuate the ignorance about it and put homosexuals at odds with one another. A major war within the homosexual community ensued because homosexuals who were able to hide behind their masculinity looked down upon those who were more obviously gay. It is very much like the war to this day remains between light-skinned and dark-skinned blacks. However, one thing I did learn from this new war in the gay community, it taught me that a man could be gay and still maintain his masculine characteristics. This was a huge discovery for me because it was the first time I realized that there were men who chose not to act effeminate which helped keep their homosexuality a secret. On the other hand, I also began noticing that there were some men who were innately effeminate, but who did not indulge or desire homosexual activities at all. Although it is true that some do.

For many years I wondered why I still had never desired having sexual relations with females. By the age of 29, I had tried everything in the lifestyle I was taught to believe in, yet I also wanted to change so desperately. My life had always felt empty and worthless, and by this point my inner soul was crying out for help and I truly felt that no man knew the void I had. I didn't know how to go about a change. After seeking sexual relationships with various men on a daily basis with no fulfillment I decided to pray for help. I would pray to God to please free me from the sins of this world. However, even with my new prayer life I still had the desire to have sexual relationships with various men. It didn't matter who the guys were. It was like being addicted to drugs. I just couldn't stop. It didn't even matter if I had to pay for sex. My prayer life continued to grow and one day I recall the spirit of God began speaking to me telling me to find a church so I could get the spiritual teachings that would help me change. I wanted desperately to be obedient and honor God's request that I find a church home, but unfortunately for me I did not obey until I had finally moved and settled in Washington, D.C. As for now my life would continue to be surrounded by drama as it always had.

THE WORLD OF MADNESS

Around the time I was deciding whether to relocate to our nation's capital, Debbie, the former Miss Morehouse and I became very good friends. She had asked for my help and it was my pleasure to support her dream of becoming a Hollywood actress, although I never really felt that she had the special quality my baby sister had to become a big name in the entertainment industry. Unlike others, this Miss Morehouse never displayed true talent but she did have a wonderful personality and in many ways that in itself could take her far in the industry. As the first Miss Black Collegiate winner, Debbie had acquired lots of exposure and after graduating from Spelman College she wanted to take advantage of all of the doors that had opened to her. The one thing I will never forget is the determination she had as a person. I loved the confidence she displayed which always made me think of a flamboyant homosexual with something to prove. I really admired her confidence because it was something I wished I had as a homosexual. In many ways she wasn't the most feminine young woman I'd ever met but she did have beauty unlike other young ladies in the entertainment world. I really felt deep down in my heart that she was gay because she never exhibited an attraction for the opposite sex nor had she been known to date men.

Knowing I was having difficulty trying to decide if I would actually move to D.C., in order to live a more active homosexual lifestyle, Debbie asked me to move to Los Angeles with her to pursue an entertainment career. Even with my past desire to be a professional dancer, by this time, even I wanted nothing to do with the entertainment industry. Rather, it was in my heart to learn more about the exciting homosexual lifestyle I had heard so much about and begin to try to find some happiness in my life. Needless to say, I did wind up moving to Washington, D.C., and Debbie headed to Los Angeles, ultimately becoming the actress she so desired to be. I proudly celebrated her success when I saw her in the first movie she starred in with Kidd-n-Play. Most recently she had a role in a movie starring recording artist LA Reid. Debbie had several roles in TV sitcoms, and I was always amazed at the incredible roles she landed. I was really shocked when a popular black women's magazine featured her as well. The article portrayed her as a beautiful up and coming starlet, in spite of the fact that I could not recall Debbie being so talented. Debbie was now living the life I had wanted so badly for my baby sister, and I recognized that it took determination and persistence on her part to succeed in the mad entertainment world.

I found my success being a part of a world full of handsome homosexuals who spent much of their time doing drugs in hopes of forgetting the life they took part in. I wondered had the heterosexual world driven homosexuals to live this type of promiscuous lifestyle that sometimes led to a death from disease or overdosing on drugs. Although the homosexual lifestyle had an open arms policy to the lost and struggling homosexual, the reality was that so many were having sex with anonymous partners. With all that taking place around me, the dismal truth of it all didn't change my outlook on homosexuality. Many years would pass before I would recognize that I was not happy with the disgusting life I had chosen to live.

Down the road it would become clear that while this lifestyle had many dysfunctional issues, because there was nowhere to go to discuss openly my desire to be set free from this trap, I remained bound far longer than I wanted to. However, not knowing any better I arrived in D.C., excited about the prospects of my new life and those I would meet who shared similarities with me. No one told me that living this seemingly wonderful homosexual existence had such horrible consequences. While I was excited to be around others like me, I did have moments when I questioned things like, would I ever find true love and had I been correct in giving up my college education at Morehouse College? In the end, what I would figure out was that my new lifestyle was all a mirage and the reality of it was that I'd continued to face rejection. Only now the rejection would come from the many one-night stands that would constitute my love life. I would also learn that the constant battle I had inside myself would be magnified by a whole new set of abuses that I'd face in my adult life. As a child the abuse was much different because back then my abusers had physical and mental power over me, but as an adult I would endure abuse at my own hands because I would trust those who got me to believe they actually loved me. It was normal in this lifestyle for someone to say they loved you today and not acknowledge your existence after they had sexual relations with you. This was normal behavior for homosexuals because many didn't know how to define love between two men. In the end there is no definition for an abnormal intimate relationship between two men.

Many homosexual men judged their sexual partners by appearance which explained why so many became victim to the deadly AIDS virus. People were all of a sudden dying because they gave in to a hot steamy moment that had absolutely nothing to do with LOVE. This was hitting the homosexual community hard and because many heterosexuals were not honest about their own sexuality, AIDS quickly crossed over to the heterosexual community hitting them even harder. So many bi-sexual and gay men were trying to live normal lives but were really in the closet. As they lived in two worlds, AIDS began to spread quickly to heterosexual women and their unborn babies. In many ways, no one accepted responsibility for their behavior and the damage it was causing throughout the world.

Once AIDS hit, I found that deep inside I didn't want to be a part of the homosexual lifestyle any longer, but my new homosexual friends had taught me how to be strong and stand up for our community. Even if I had wanted to get out, I convinced myself that it was better to stay because I certainly could not go back to the heterosexual world for acceptance and understanding. In many ways, it was they who had led me to seek out homosexual freedom in order to finally get away from the cruelty I faced in their world. I began to tighten my boot straps and dive in headfirst. I began to believe all the hype about being born gay and being this way because God created me as such. Deep down inside, however, I thought how closely this lifestyle compared to the biblical cities of Sodom and Gomorrah; the two cities God destroyed because of the horrendous perversions taking place there.

If all my friends had been honest they, too, would have admitted that the lifestyle was unbearable and the only way they were able to endure it was by partaking in substance abuse. Not unlike when my father drank to cover up his pain when I was a child, I knew that in order to deal with the reality of homosexuality, one had to cover it up with alcohol or drugs. I found that I became a difficult person to be around, as I had developed the compulsion to debate with others. I believe I wanted the power that came from having a voice and being heard, so I began to find joy in trying to get people to explain things they believed in only to try and confuse them with their own views. I especially loved debating with heterosexuals because they had been the source of so much of my pain. In most cases I usually walked away from them after making them feel flustered as they struggled to answer a question I knew they could not answer. Sometimes I would debate with other homosexuals about their views on being gay, and found that the only final answer they could usually come up with was it was simply their life.

Many, many, times as I walked actively in my homosexual lifestyle I considered leaving it behind, but the struggle inside my mind was unbearable at times. I wondered where else I would go, and with nowhere being the answer I remained bonded to the gay community continually seeking ways to find enjoyment in it. I did enjoy the company of many of my homosexual friends because of their uniqueness and strength to overcome the demons of their inner struggle. In a lot of ways we appeared to have so much in common, but truthfully some never appeared to suffer from low self-esteem like me. While I often suffered from self-loathing deep down inside, many of my friends identified my struggles as result of a deep depression. Many homosexuals saw me as strange, and having a friendship with me was not always welcomed by other homosexuals. I even hated myself at times because I didn't know how to just live, and I continued to blame my abusers for my inability to fit in anywhere. I think about all the many children who must be experiencing what I went through as a child. As a child without a voice I chose not to speak for long periods of time in order to avoid persecution from others who made me feel inhuman and empty. I knew that I was not the only homosexual who suffered with bouts of emptiness, but it seemed that other homosexuals didn't ever admit their true feelings openly. Much of the pain was covered up by our outward feminine behaviors and jesters which were exhibited to convince outsiders that we had the confidence needed to overcome the outside world.

My life as an African American homosexual man set me

back even further with trying to gain self-acceptance. I had not only faced persecution in church, and the heterosexual world at large, but now I was faced with the discrimination I was told existed by the white homosexual community as well. Trying to understand the separation between black and white homosexual worlds made my life even that much more confusing. I found that I enjoyed spending time with white people, in particular white homosexuals, because I personally received some acceptance from them. Although the white homosexual world was very different from ours, I never required the approval of white men straight or gay because around them I no longer felt I had to compete for attention or measure up to their high standards. Although white homosexuals were discriminated against from their white counterparts in the heterosexual community, they in turn tended to discriminate against African American homosexuals. So to put it in a nutshell, the race card also crossed over into the homosexual community. I can't explain why, but I genuinely was not sexually attracted to men outside my race.

I admired the way in which the white homosexual community united together to support a cause. Because most of my pain was inflicted by the African American community, I thought about joining forces with the white community because it seemed easier for me to deal with my struggles that way. However, deep down inside I knew I could never become intimate with a white male; although I despised most black men due to the pain I identified with them, I still had the kind of attraction for black men that black woman did. It was like a love/hate relationship. I hated them for how they verbally and physically raped my body and soul as a child, yet on the other hand they exemplified strength and great passion and I desired that from them. I recall as a child watching movies about slavery like *Roots*, and seeing slave masters rape men and women of color, stealing their souls and bodies, but yet most slaves remained loyal. This is the type of bondage I found

76

myself in with black men.

Although black men were my abusers from age five, I found myself participating willingly with confusion. Yet there were those times I didn't want to partake in sexual immorality with my abusers. At times I cried and pleaded for the molestation to end but the perpetrators would ignore my pleas until they were satisfied. Even with the utter disgust of things taking place with me I often allowed myself to find peace in knowing that God would rescue me from the shame and guilt I carried from day to day. Each day would start like the one before not knowing how it would end, although when the sun would set I could celebrate knowing I had made it through yet another day. For many years as a child I spent my life like a slave to my own body, wondering if I would ever be free. That which my body took part in controlled my mind and kept me in shackles and chains.

I recall the times I sought freedom in my mind but I could always hear voices screaming loudly inside my head. Even as an adult I struggled to be free inside my mind, but freedom would not fully come until I realized that only the power of God could set me free from the chains of bondage. My search for God came full circle upon my arrival to Washington, D.C. It was then that I remembered God had once told me to seek out a church home so I could be taught his word. Hearing this again from God, I quickly sought out a church that I had heard about from several friends. The Greater Holy Church in Washington, D.C., was popular because of its pastor and co-pastor. People everywhere celebrated attending this church and spoke of how their lives had been changed after giving their lives to Christ and remaining under their teachings. Once I began attending, I learned how important my salvation was and how much I needed a church home, but most importantly I enjoyed the teachings of Bishop Allen and Co-Pastor Shirley Oswell. After joining this new church, I immediately noticed how much better I felt, and I also experienced a change taking over my life. The biblical teachings by Bishop Allen Oswell and Co-Pastor Shirley Oswell helped me to establish a more grounded relationship with God, something I had always heard others talk about but never experienced for myself. I quickly came to understand the meaning of John 3:16: For God so loved the world that he gave his only begotten son. This meant that God loved me in spite of how others treated me. Knowing this created a true desire in me to continue searching for God and his purposed in my life.

That Which I Feared the Most

I thought about all the years of pain that could have been resolved had I only known to seek out the biblical teachings which showed me how to go about healing my soul and spirit. For many years I had heard people talking about spirituality, and I even recall that as a young teen how I favored gospel artists like James Cleveland and Tramaine Hawkins. While most families attended church on Sundays, I spent many Sunday's listening to 8-track tapes and albums of gospel music. I felt so much peace while singing and meditating on the music being played. During those times my spirit had a connection with this higher power many people spoke of, not knowing that this was actually God summoning me so he could heal my soul. My relatives spent much of their time on the weekends drinking, playing cards, gambling, and fighting. My father relied on weekends to come so he could go on drinking binges and use them as an excuse to physically abuse my mother. As a child I can not recall a weekend where my father did not get drunk and abuse my mother physically and verbally. Because we were the youngest of the six children, my sisters and I felt much of the impact of the abuse because we didn't understand. Although my brothers were older, they still were not strong enough to stop my father's abuse. But, it was a blessing when my three older brothers finally got big enough to stop my father from inflicting his abuse on our mother. While most children enjoyed the weekends, my sisters and I hated to see the weekends come because they meant my father would become this drunken maniac who was completely out of control beating my mom from Friday to Sunday each and every weekend. It was as if we didn't know him because when he was sober he was such a wonderful person. I will never forget how my father beat my mother like she was a child while their children looked on helplessly. I loved my mother so much because she worked so hard to give us the little things in life. Sometimes the abuse was too much for her and she would leave my father or have the local police remove him from the home. My father was never gone for any real length of time, two or three weeks at the most. He would always be allowed to return because of the way he pleaded with my mom for forgiveness. I can't explain the love my mom had for my father but she always found a way to forgive him, even though she knew his abusive behavior would return. My mother often talked about her desire to keep our family together, not wanting us to grow up without our father. Unlike today, keeping families together was very important back then. My father was truly a hard worker and a good provider for his family. Although we didn't have much money, my father made sure his children always had food on the table. But even as a great provider I certainly didn't enjoy the painful psychological damage he caused our family to endure. Even though I was only a child, I still felt it may have been better for us to live without him because of the abuse. When he would become abusive to my mother, I hated him, most times wishing he were dead. My father would often make promises to his family that he would seek treatment for his addiction, but needless to say it never happened. Seeking counseling was virtually unheard of for black people in those days. One of the reasons black people drank was because so many faced poverty. In many ways drinking was therapy and counseling especially for black men. Some say that the 1960's and early 1970's was an era of depression, especially for black men who felt the pressures of trying to provide for their families in a prejudice world. This time was the height of the exodus of black men away from their wives and children, due to a feeling of worthlessness at the inability to provide adequately for them. Black families without a father present tended to do okay on welfare, making the father obsolete, and has led us to where we are today having black men completely out of their children's lives. What started as depression in the black community has led to the absence of fathers in the home which is now considered normal.

The depression evident in my home was made even worse by my father's drinking. I never will forget how my mother sometimes went to work with black eyes from being kicked in the face by my father. She always appeared so strong, never showing any signs of pain or any weakness. No one deserved to live through that kind of abuse, especially not my mother or her children. This part of our lives was torture at its worst. The abuse was always worse when my father got so out of control he'd get out his 35 millimeter handgun and threatened to kill my mother and anyone who got in the way. Sometimes the children did get in the way by trying to convince him to put the gun away, but most of the time my sisters and I just ran for cover screaming, crying, and hiding in rooms and closets, afraid of being shot by the loaded gun. It seemed like families everywhere including our neighbors and relatives endured similar kinds of abuse in their homes.

I recall Seth, an older cousin, who tried to stop his father from beating his mother, my mother's sister. The story I have been privy to is that my uncle pulled out a gun, and he and Seth got into a tussle which left my uncle with several fatal gunshot wounds. I recall the telephone call we received and the caller telling my mother that Uncle Seth, Sr. had been shot. We'd later find out that Seth, Jr. was the one who pulled the trigger.

By the time my family arrived on the scene, my uncle's body was being taken out of the house by the medical examiner in a black body bag. This left both families in turmoil. I had hoped, even though I was only a child, others would learn from the tragic death of my uncle but, unfortunately this tragedy didn't even change my own father's behavior.

My sisters and I had always vowed that we would never drink because of what we saw alcohol do to our father. Oddly, as the years passed I recall that my mother began standing up to my father by fighting back. I loved her courage as she tried to prove to my father that enough was enough by finding whatever she could use as a weapon to protect herself against his attacks. She at least was going to make him think first about hitting her. I knew she had to start fighting back in order to survive the abuse, because things were really out of control by this time. One thing had changed because of her new courage, my father thought hard about the battles he picked with my mom because he knew he'd now have a battle on his hands. When my mother began to fight back, my parents fought like cats and dogs. I often wondered where she got her strength from to fight my father. Their fights were real like the ones shown by the World Wrestling Federation. I don't even think my mother knew where her strength came from but she proved that women could find strength when they needed it. Most of the children I knew in the neighborhood had single mothers or mothers with live-in boyfriends, so they rarely witnessed the physical and verbal abuses that my mother and aunts did. When abuse took place at the hands of a live-in boyfriend, the police would just remove him from the home. Boyfriends could easily be replaced so removal was the action of choice in most cases. Today, many women hold lucrative jobs and have changed their attitude towards needing a man in their lives. With this financial advantage, many black women today no longer have to endure abuse at the hands of a man. With women's liberation and the new woman's movement, many women don't see themselves as being submissive wives as the Bible commands. Rather, they see themselves as equal partners, because of the financial power they bring to the marriage. Many women are also content to have children without being married; I have very strong feelings about the fact that so many are being raised without fathers around. While most people profess God is in their lives, they don't honor the sanctity of marriage which is sanctioned by God. As a homosexual, watching and listening to the behaviors of many heterosexual couples regarding relationships, it was clear that their lives were no better than mine. Yet many heterosexuals have criticized and tried pointing their fingers at me back then about my lifestyle.

WHAT ABOUT RELIGION?

When we were young, my mother didn't require my brothers and sisters to attend church or follow a spiritual path. As a child I envied other children whose parents demanded that they attended Sunday church services. In many ways it defined family unity, something my family didn't seem to have. There were many families who went to church that I felt God wanted me to spend time with, but church for me never went beyond meditating and listening to gospel music on Sundays. In looking back over my life, I surely missed the times I spent listening to gospel music as a young teenager. I found peace in those times of meditation.

As I have said, being young with no direction as a homosexual left me empty and in need of spiritual guidance. This doesn't offer any real explanation for those who grew up in the church and still ended up living actively in the homosexual lifestyle. Perhaps it is just another example of how churches remain reluctant to deal with the root spirit of homosexuality when they see it. Knowing what I know today, had I gotten professional counseling or began taking antidepressants, I would probably be in more pain than before I started treatment. I feel this way because counseling would have attempted to get me to change my homosexual thoughts.

How could counseling change me when no one knows why people are homosexual, especially for someone like me who feels they are homosexual only because of the molesting experienced as a child? Why would I want to be counseled into coming to terms with being homosexual when living this lifestyle has been empty and unfulfilling; a life of constant battling and dealing with self-loathing and unending turmoil? How can anyone try to get us to be comfortable in this lifestyle, when loving relationships between homosexual men are usually non-existent? It was better that I waited on God rather than endure years and years of therapy which would undoubtedly fail at changing me. God takes his children just as they are and then he makes the changes needed. We only have to give him that chance.

It would take the power of God to help me see the homosexual life I had accepted was bringing me to the brink of destruction. While exploring I struggled with having to pay men for sex, accepting noncommittal sexual relationships, and living a life of one-night stands. This hardly defined love or a healthy life. Many homosexual men express the same feelings. Many will admit that while they do have strong sexual desires for men, they know in reality that committed relationships are virtually impossible to obtain. If having sex could keep people together most people would not have a problem keeping the same partner for a lifetime. Relationships are much more than just participating in sexual relations, which is why same-sex relationships often lack the ingredients to succeed.

Many homosexuals will deny the biblical truth about homosexuality. There is no sound doctrine showing long lasting and committed relationships between homosexuals. It may sound like I am bashing homosexuals but from one who has lived the lifestyle; I only want to help set people free. I don't speak against the homosexual, I simply speak against the unhealthiness of the lifestyle. Human emotions have caused many people to make many mistakes. What the homosexual feels is real, but acting on these feelings is what isn't healthy. We will always be battling inside our flesh about making personal choices. There is no doubt, the struggle of homosexuality is real without question, but the real question is how will you be able to face God if you don't change your actions?

Seeking God & True Salvation

After God led me to Greater Holy Church in Washington, D.C., I learned things I had never known about the Bible. Beforehand, I had only been taught by preachers and churchgoers that because I was gay I was going to go to hell. How could that be when it was not a lifestyle I had wanted? Even so, what many didn't know was that I had always felt like I was already living in hell. Many homosexuals feel this way. I recall a conversation I had with my brother who had molested me. He had become involved in church and told me one day that I needed to change my lifestyle. It was hard for me to understand how he could condemn my behavior when he was one of the reasons I had ended up in my homosexual struggle. I thought it was a shame how this brother never apologized for what he had done to me when he molested my body and soul.

Bishop Oswell was the one clergy who believed that struggling with homosexuality was no different than anyone else's sinful struggle. I enjoyed how open and bold the bishop was as he ministered the Gospel to the congregation. He taught me that I could not continue in my sin because it was unacceptable to God to live in sin. I also learned that Jesus had died to take my sins away. I recall how something registered inside that made me want to change immediately. This was a real life-altering moment for me. Because of learning and believing the Gospel of Jesus, I was beginning to feel powerful. I felt like I finally had some control of my life, and it would get even better if I just learned to apply the teachings of Jesus Christ. I understood that I had the power to change all of the time because of the power of God in me. I just didn't know it. It was then that I understood why churchgoers felt so powerful after attending church services. For me, this was a new beginning in my life. I finally felt that I had hope, something no one had ever offered before, not even after I had attended the Sex Anonymous Sex Addiction classes I had tried earlier. I often left those classes as empty as I had arrived. Of course, this was the one solution that most gay communities offered to help with their struggles. While I did appreciate that they tried to reach out to the community, the classes weren't happening for me.

While many in the gay community bought into being OUT, few actual went to church to find true inner peace because of being ridiculed by "holier than thou" churchgoers. Greater Holy Church was particularly known for having a large population of homosexuals. I felt very comfortable being a church member there, because I knew there were several people who understood my struggle and could identify with my pain.

Unfortunately, competition among homosexual churchgoers was at an all-time high, and to fit in those who had a talent flaunted it in order to help them be more accepted. Homosexual members who could sing were acknowledged most, even by the pastors, yet others were scorned. This proves my earlier point, that if pastors, ministers, and other religious leaders, showed mercy towards all homosexuals in the body of Christ, then the world at large would be more tolerant of them. This is not too much to ask because we all need mercy.

Bishop T.D. Jakes is one minister to be applauded. His ministry is truly about helping all people who are hurting. He tries to help with any and all sin; anywhere there is pain. I will never forget attending one of the Man Power conferences where Bishop Jakes taught that "you may have done it, but, you are not what you've done." What a powerful statement! That statement alone is enough to draw on daily.

It is very important to understand that we are what God says we are and not what people say we are. If leaders would get to the place where they recognize that all human beings are imperfect, and are nothing without God's grace, then we all would be accepted by the church. Bishop T. D. Jakes teaches that there are weaknesses even in the best of us. On the other hand, there is good even in the worst of us. Life is about having a peace of God which surpasses all understanding and knowing that God loves us all. This is what healing is all about. It is God that allows a change to take place in each of us, however even before that change comes God requires that we love each other.

While living in Washington, D.C., and continuing to attend church my life became more profound. Of all the places I've lived in, Washington, D.C., is the city I will never forget. It is not just the beautiful nation's capital, at that time it was also the capital for black gays at that time. Most people were fully aware that D.C. was the homosexual capital for blacks, although most homosexuals were living on what they called the "DL" down low (not openly living the gay lifestyle). Because so many black gay men lived in D.C., most people automatically assumed that if you were a black male your sexual preference went either way. Most females didn't seem to be bothered by all the madness. Washington, D.C., was indeed the place for men, in particular, to live out their secret lives. I wish I could have grown up in a city like this because I might have lived without being so harshly judged. This is not to say that people there condoned homosexuality, but because of the large population of homosexuals, one had more support from their peers there. Even though I felt that I was finally free from judgmental people, I still suffered from social anxiety disorder and from the inner pain caused in my childhood. As free as I felt, I still didn't feel at peace inside, because I knew that the spirit of homosexuality still didn't allow me to have peace with God. Although many gays felt liberated in D.C., I am sure they still experienced spells of emptiness deep inside.

QUEST FOR GAY LOVE

When I first relocated to D.C. my life spun out of control. I tried to convince myself that I could change my situation by hiding, even though most people knew my truth just by looking at me. I wanted to find a man to love me so I began a quest that would be somewhat difficult since I didn't do social events, parties, or nightclubs due to my panic attacks. I would panic at the thought of others judging me and I also didn't like being around men who confessed openly to being gay because I saw this as a clear sign of them showing their weaknesses. Most men in my past had been strong and very independent, and because of all these things my quest for love would be difficult indeed.

I typically didn't judge men on their size, height, or complexion; however, I only dated African American men. The men I encountered most were financially secure, which was an indication to me that they were only seeking sexual release and not a committed relationship. Many of the men I was involved with never really saw themselves as homosexual and I believe they saw me the way most men always had, just someone to take advantage of. This quickly let me know that I had to change the game so I decided to change my image. I had always been such a small guy with my weight staying around

125 pounds, so I began exercising and lifting weights. I thought by doing this I would appear more masculine and less like a candidate for the wolves to take advantage of. Within two years my appearance had changed dramatically, as did my image (or so I thought). My perception of myself was that since I had physically changed then I somehow seemed different to others. My friends, however, shared with me that I still acted the same, so of course my ego was crushed even more. I had been striving to achieve a total image change, hoping to find a way to get rid of the effeminate behavior I had acquired as a child. My background in dance seemed to have enhanced it even more, so even though I suddenly looked very masculine, I was still the feminine little boy who I despised.

Searching for friends in the gay community turned out to be a difficult task. Heterosexuals seemed to find friends based on various common interests but when a homosexual wants to befriend someone there is usually drama involved in some form. It is difficult to function outside of the gay community because heterosexuals are not very comfortable being befriended by homosexuals. Most straight people think homosexuals will poison or contaminate them in some way, so they run at the thought of having a homosexual as a friend. Because of this, homosexuals usually befriend one another which is often difficult as well because the only thing most homosexuals have in common are the demons they battle. On the other hand homosexual friendships can also be somewhat of an encouragement because each person can identify with the struggles of the other. I found that for me, befriending another homosexual was challenging because it is difficult for two broken vessels to mend each other. So while I continued trying to adjust to my new lifestyle, things around me began to fall apart.

But my God

shall supply

all your need

according to

his riches

in glory by

Christ Jesus.

Philippians 4:19

Tragedy - vs. - Faith

The sudden illness of my baby sister was a shock to me as well as to my entire family. In midsummer of 1993, she began suffering from reoccurring bouts with yeast infections and unexplained weight loss. Weight had always been an issue for her, especially during the time she competed in pageants when keeping her weight down was a challenge, but in 1993 Robin began losing weight without dieting. Large amounts of weight had begun to drop off her frame, so much weight that it caused the family to worry.

My sister had held several professional job positions in the Midwest and wanted to move closer north, so she moved to Allentown, PA, where she had landed a high paying executive job with a major corporation. Deep down I wanted her to move west to pursue Hollywood, but I guess she'd had enough of the entertainment world and she decided to move east instead. It was nice to have her closer to me, as I was still in Washington, D.C., at that time, and could visit her more often. My sister's career allowed her to buy a beautiful home and drive a Jaguar. She truly had found a good life for herself in Allentown. During that time I even had the conversation with her about my lifestyle and while in no way did she condone it, she loved me and supported me. I tried to do the same thing for her when she revealed that she had been dating a married man who had not committed to leaving his wife. Although her lover seemed to be an okay guy, I had a difficult time accepting that he was married and dating my sister. It seemed that my sister's love life as well as her health was suffering greatly but she continued to work and enjoy the fruits of her labor.

Because the yeast infections continued to reoccur, my baby sister was referred to a dermatologist who told her that she needed to be tested for the HIV/AIDS virus. This would explain the yeast infections and the drastic drop in weight that had finally made her look anorexic. I remember the call from my sister telling me that she had to be tested for that deadly virus. I went into shock but had to remain calm in order to console her as she cried uncontrollably. Like with all families, tragedy hit mine but hit it hard. When I finally saw my baby sister, she was shockingly thin. It made me think about the time Oprah Winfrey had lost a large amount of weight, and the show she did where she rolled out animal fat equaling the amount of weight she had lost. Oprah was so proud of herself on that show, but the problem was that she had dropped the weight so quickly that her new look shocked the world with her drastic weight loss. She looked like a beautiful model. My sister looked this same shocking way. Oprah would go on to put her weight back on, but my sister would never get that chance. Robin fought her disease with the same fight she gave everything else she did. I loved my sister and found it ironic that she would contract the very disease that had once been labeled the gay man's disease. Life is not easy to figure out. All we can do is try to accept those things we cannot change and try to live as best we can in spite of them. It was extremely hard to accept tragedy when it kept coming to plague my family. Unfortunately for us, tragedy would not just stop with the suffering of my sister.

After learning that my baby sister had AIDS my faith was shaken, yet I had not totally abandoned God. My brother had already revealed much earlier that he was suffering from the AIDS virus, which wasn't as much a shock to me since he was the brother who had molested me as a child. My brother suffered greatly and ultimately died in a hospice. I was upset at my father for this because I felt dying in a hospice was a cruel place for a child to die, but my father didn't understand the disease when it pertained to a man. My brother was treated very differently in his pain than my sister would be treated later. But, I really loved my sister and was glad that she wasn't alone. Although I had known many people that had died from this dreadful disease, no one close to me had until the death of my brother which was almost unbearable. I was truly frightened for my baby sister because not only was Robin my best friend; she meant the world to me.

Death continued to stalk us, and it was a blow to us when we received the call that yet another brother had been found dead of a brain aneurysm. I found it very hard to believe all these things that were happening so fast. I handled the stress by seeking out love from men in the same way I did as a child, but of course I knew I had to be strong for my baby sister so I flew home to attend my brother's funeral to support her. In 1993, I really believed that the treatments for HIV/AIDS had advanced, especially since it was around the time that NBA star Magic Johnson announced he had HIV. But, to my surprise we soon discovered that my sister not only had the HIV virus but she had full-blown AIDS. After this discovery, she found it hard to face the world and her friends which was sad because while the world showed compassion for Magic Johnson it showed little compassion for those without celebrity status who were suffering from this disease. After a long painful struggle my sister, Robin P. Sipp, passed away in the summer of 1994. This was truly the saddest day of my life.

I always feared that my life would end in death from contracting AIDS because of the homosexual lifestyle I lived. This was the time where people were warned to abstain from sex for fear of contracting and/or spreading this deadly disease, but most people ignored this plea. I continued to indulge in sex and in 1991, I decided to get tested. I was so grateful when my results returned negative. Most gays rejected being tested because of the fear they had of the outcome. After I learned of my negative status, I vowed I would never be tested again because of the panic and fear I experienced while waiting the two weeks for my results. Although I vowed I would never have homosexual relations again and put myself at risk for contracting AIDS I would not honor this vow.

This time in my life had been very stressful. In a short span of time I had buried two brothers and my baby sister, and although I continued to walk with God and keep my faith I also continued to behave very irresponsibly. My prayer was for God to continue to protect me from myself. I often thought about how hypocritical my life had become. I was a Christian who continued to partake in the life of a homosexual. I honestly felt my life was being controlled by a power much stronger than myself, because I should have known that even with watching my sister and brothers painful and humiliating deaths I still could not break the stronghold over my life. I knew that I would have to pray harder and hold on to God closer than I ever had. In my heart I loved God more than myself, but found this difficult to prove because it was so easy for me to slip back into my sinful ways.

PECKED TO DEATH - THEY WANT ME

People back in Daytona Beach began to spread cruel talk that my family had been cursed and was getting what we deserved. Many even said that my family had a plague and encouraged others to stay away from us. The one thing that most people could not understand was how this disease bypassed me since I was the "faggot." They certainly could have understood it if I had died. While I found their words to be hurtful and sad, they didn't surprise me because those spewing these awful things were the same people who had caused me so much pain as a child and although their words stung they didn't have the same impact on me as they once had. This is when I understood that people didn't have the power over me that I thought they had, God was the only one who had true power and God was inside of me. This meant I had power as well. I could now look my harassers in the face and smile and say, "God be with you." In many ways I felt vindicated, yet guilty because I did feel that I should have died rather than my baby sister. I could look in my parents' eyes and feel their hurt and loss. I even recall hearing my father say that he did not understand why God had taken his baby girl away. My parents both felt helpless because of losing three children in three short years. The only joy I had was in knowing that my older sister Vanessa had started a family and had given birth to a beautiful little girl. Just before my sister died, Vanessa was pregnant again with her second child which happened to be a little boy. These new lives were a sure sign that God was still in control in the face of all the death around us.

My father took my baby sister's death very hard and suffered greatly because of it. He was just not the same and would never be again. Not only was Robin the pride and joy of my life, but she also was equally as special to my father. Tragedy struck again when my father was soon after diagnosed with cancer but refused treatment because he felt that life was not worth living without his baby girl. During his illness, I made a habit of calling my dad every week but he never gave me any indication of how sick he really was. So, when I received a call from my mother informing me that my dad had been admitted into the hospital it was hard for me to digest. That was on a Wednesday and the following Sunday morning my dad died. His death saddened me so much that it put me on the path that led me to a new life in Atlanta, Georgia. I felt that with all the loss I had experienced I needed to be closer to my remaining family.

Because I had heard about the "new" Atlanta I was excited about my move. Washington, D.C., was getting old and I was tired of the emptiness that came from the string of sexual encounters I subjected myself to with so many Mr. Wrongs. My biggest regret about moving away was leaving my church, Greater Holy Calvary. This was the church that had helped give my life its spiritual foundation, even though I continued to slip back into the sins of the lifestyle. I had found a relationship with God but it was obvious that our relationship was not as strong as it was when I first found him. The truth was that I had begun walking away from the intimate relationship that God and I had. It's amazing how when I first found God I didn't care who accepted me, but my need to be loved by others caused me to regress in my relationship with God. I think it injured me further to continue attending church and finally realizing that people there were no different than those in the world. I found that churchgoers had no intention of receiving the struggling homosexual, so I lost interest in attending church. When I first started attending, everyone appeared to have so much love and willingness to accept the newly saved Christian. What I didn't understand was why they didn't know how to truly forgive once they found out that that newly saved Christian was also a struggling homosexual. Although God had already forgiven me, I still sought validation from others and this caused me to fall away from church because church folk seemed incapable of forgiving with their true heart. The Bible asks: "How can you love God whom you have never seen, but hate your brother whom you see every day?" This is ringed so true to me and I figured that I would never understand the heart of a churchgoer.

Although Christians are taught to be like Christ, most only condemn in the way Jesus was condemned. Keeping my eyes on them took my eyes off of God, and caused me to slip further away from the intimate relationship I had established with him early on. In my seven-year walk with God I realized that most people were as lost as I was yet they didn't know it. I started getting offended when someone brought my sinful lifestyle to my attention, and I now understood why people got upset when the preacher taught on sin; no one wants to really face the wrongs in their life. However, it is only when we face our sins that we can ask God's forgiveness for them. The healing comes when God forgives and replaces the sinful behavior with something holy. Unfortunately, most Christians see their relationship with God as being equivalent to the position they hold in church. The fakeness of many churchgoers was a reality check for me, which was all I needed to convince myself that I was only going to church out of routine. This was enough of an excuse to cause me to slip deeper into my old sinful ways.

The constant flow of negatives in my life made the decision

to move to Atlanta that much easier for me. Once I finally made the decision to move I began selling my personal belongings and making preparations by contacting friends in Atlanta. My break from Washington, D.C., was not easy, as it was very painful for me to inform my pastors that I would be moving back south. This was painful because this man and woman of God had given me a new direction which introduced me to a spiritual life. This was a very emotional time for me, because I always felt that Bishop Oswell was my spiritual father and understood my pain and my struggles with homosexuality. He had taught me all he could about the life God desired for his children, but like most people the bishop really didn't know how homosexuality could be corrected and could only tell me to abstain from having sex. No one had yet discovered a pill to fix homosexuals like they had with so many other inflictions. I always admired those homosexuals who could suppress their homosexuality, although I knew they weren't cured. Many gay men who believed in the Bible could change their homosexual desires, but faced much criticism from the gay community. Some homosexuals really don't believe it is possible to change their desires. Although many homosexuals attend church on a regular basis and study the biblical teachings of God, they still practice homosexual lifestyles. The church still does not know how to help the homosexual, but I personally believed that God would change my homosexual desires if I would only make the effort to meet him halfway.

GOD'S GIFT TO MAN

Leaving Washington, D.C., was also difficult for another reason. Not long after moving to D.C., I had met and bonded with someone who became like a brother to me. Deion was my dream brother because he was the only person outside my real family who meant a lot to me. I loved this guy even more than any of my birth brothers, and I will never forget how we met. It was in the late 1980's during a muggy summer day in D.C. It was a busy day at the Boys and Girls Fitness Center where I was working out and admiring him from afar, because he was such an attractive young man. When I first saw him I noticed how everyone else in the gym seemed to be admiring him as well. Deion had an incredible physique, the kind of body that every guy dreamed of having. His only flaw, if you could call it that, was that he was only 5 foot 7 inches tall. After I got to know him, I'd overhear people (both gay and straight) talking about him like he was a local celebrity. Even my best friend at that time, who happened to be gay, mentioned a guy he had noticed walking around town captivating the lunch crowd in downtown Washington, D.C. I later found out that the guy he had spoken of was Deion. Deion had become very aware of the much unwanted attention he was receiving from male and female admirers and because he was straight, he certainly did not honor the outward adulation he was receiving from homosexuals.

One of my deepest desires was to have a heterosexual friend and be treated like a normal person by him, but I never thought any heterosexual guy would be interested in being my friend especially one who looked like Deion. Before we formally met, I would panic when I saw him in the gym and I'd actually break out in large volumes of sweat, but because I was working out no one noticed. One day, I was being harassed in the gym about being gay and was defending myself by denying the accusations. Deion automatically came to my defense, which shocked me because in all the years of my life I had never had anyone other than my sisters defend me in this way. I didn't understand what had warranted this support, but afterward he and I began training together and I guess as they say the rest is history.

Although Deion seemed fine with developing a friendship with me, his fiancée did not receive me so well. She was concerned about our relationship, because Deion and I began to spend a lot of time together. The time we spent together made me feel really special, and I could feel my self-esteem rise which caused my confidence level to rise dramatically in a short amount of time. Although we didn't discuss it, I thought Deion really knew that I was a homosexual and it just didn't matter to him. A couple of years into our friendship, I invited him to a gay club. By accepting the invitation, I thought for sure he knew about my lifestyle, but that night a bomb exploded. When we arrived at the gay club, many of the guys there automatically took notice of Deion and began flocking around and rushing in on him. This offended Deion greatly, not to mention that he began hearing rumors that began to surface about my sexuality. Deion was so upset with me that he refused to speak with me, rejecting all of my telephone calls. I was devastated by the damage caused to our relationship.

Deion and I didn't talk for approximately one year. Of

course this really damaged my self-esteem and I began to feel badly again, which lowered my self-worth tremendously. My closest gay friend took joy in the breakup of my friendship with Deion, because homosexuals often celebrate each other's downfalls; especially when a heterosexual man is involved. Our strengths were in being validated by heterosexual men. Every homosexual's dream is to have a straight man as a close friend, because having the acceptance of a straight man relieves much of the burden of being a homosexual. This is because most homosexuals really don't want to be gay and any attention given to them by a straight man makes them feel somewhat normal.

When my mom moved to Washington, D.C., Deion and I were still not talking. She had relocated because with all the tragedy she also wanted a change for her life. When she arrived, of course, she asked about Deion. I felt saddened to have to tell her that he and I were not speaking, because Deion had always called my mother, "mom." She requested that I call him so she could speak with him, and I could feel life coming back into my soul. I was happy that Deion was excited to hear from my mom, and I was elated when he suggested that he would stop by to see her. From that point on our relationship was mended and I thanked God! I promised him that I would not allow our friendship to be challenged again. Deion and I talked and he let me know that he wasn't upset that I was gay; he was upset because we had been so close and I had offended him by not sharing my innermost secret with him. I was totally in agreement with him, but explained to him that because of all the hurt I had received in my past I was not willing to risk our friendship by pushing him away with information about my lifestyle. My friendship with Deion was valuable to me because he never judged me, so I began referring to him as my brother. The time Deion and I spent together doubled. We really looked like an item but our friendship was purely based on brotherly love. I would be lying if I said that I didn't feel great passion for Deion, but I knew I could never be anything sexual to him. At any rate, God had given me a true heterosexual male friend who accepted me totally with all my flaws and I felt really blessed. All of my so-called gay friends wanted to be around Deion and would invite me to special events hoping I would bring him along, but Deion made it very clear that he was my friend and wasn't interested in being a trophy boy.

The time leading up to Deion' wedding had come fast, and I was excited about his wedding day. His fiancée was pregnant with their first child and I was invited to be a part of the wedding party as one of the ushers. Truthfully, being asked to be an usher insulted me because I couldn't understand why I had not been asked to be one of the groomsmen. I had ignored the fact that Deion had other friends that he was just as close to him as I was. For me, Deion was my best friend but he had always had other good friends along with me. Still, I was hurt to have been given such an unimportant role in his wedding and I took it so personally that I cried and moped for days. I moped so badly that I actually missed out on the wedding party dinner and rehearsals. I acted selfishly, ignoring the fact that this wedding was not about me; it was about my brother. Deion had always shown me much love and I admired the responsibility he was taking on by getting married and becoming a provider for his family. In spite of my behavior during the time of his wedding, Deion continued inviting me to his family gatherings and continued to treat me like part of his family even after he was married.

DESTRUCTION & THE POWER OF SIN

I prepared to move back to Atlanta vowing not to let anything hurt my friendship with Deion again, but before I left D.C. I broke this promise and our friendship suffered again. My homosexual lifestyle had kicked in even stronger and I allowed my sexual behaviors to get completely out of control. I believe my behavior was a result of misplaced pain I felt from losing my father, which made me so numb that I didn't care who got hurt. My brother, Deion, had asked me for an important favor and I let him down. I really didn't care about living life any longer and even though I still went to church and prayed I was just going through the motions. I knew that I was leaving unfinished business behind, but one day without apologizing to Deion I packed up my car and headed to Atlanta. I know Deion must have been truly offended when he found out I was gone, but I had retreated back into my selfish lifestyle and succumbed to the low-esteem that always found me. When I arrived in Atlanta, I thought about all I had done to damage our friendship and I tried to make amends, but Deion would not accept or return my calls. It would be two or three years later before Deion would finally speak to me, but in the end he did find it in his heart to forgive me. I am now the godfather of his son, and even though I don't get to spend a lot of time in my godson's life, it means a lot that Deion would bless me with such an honor.

I was so excited about my new start in Atlanta, and I quickly began my quest to make new friends. I was so committed to this new start that I was willing to do whatever needed to be done to prove to God that I was serious about having a starting over. I knew if I stayed focused, God would honor his promise and take care of me. First, I contacted a dear friend who I had befriended many years before. I admired this friend, who was more like a father than one of my peers, because he always stayed focused on his career and his goals. When I had left Atlanta years before, he'd had some issues with being overweight, but to my surprise when I saw him again he had lost a lot of weight and no, he was not suffering with AIDS. What he had decided to do was take serious control of his life and began a very strict fitness training program. I must admit he looked good. The only problem I saw with my staying with him was that he lived more than 40 miles outside of Atlanta. Atlanta had changed and I had not taken into account how much it had grown since the 1996 Olympics. My concern was that I was driving an old Nissan 280zx, and knowing that most employment opportunities would probably be in the city of Atlanta I feared my car might not have the stamina to handle the daily distance driving from his house to the city. I was pretty focused however on what I needed to do upon arriving to this fast paced city, and I was determined to make some real progress in my new hometown. I found a fitness center because training was still one of my priorities and I wanted to look physically fit since it helped me to somewhat hide my homosexuality.

It was not long before God took a back seat to my desires and one night, as I was leaving the fitness club, I decided to take a ride to the most popular gay strip in midtown Atlanta. I remembered from the early 1980's that this gay cruise spot was very popular, and since I didn't go out to many gay bars due to my social anxiety disorder I frequented various gay cruise spots instead. These places were very convenient, because the men who cruised them wanted the same thing I did. Things had changed a lot on the strip. It had become a place where guys could go to sell their bodies for extra income; however, back in the early 1980's men cruised the strip solely to find free sex. I really enjoyed these spots because many of the guys that walked the strip were straight or straight acting. This was right up my alley. I loved these kinds of guys because I loved that they seemed to be so strong. Some homosexuals enjoy guys, who appear to be weak or feminine, but I preferred a stronger male image; I think this was because I felt very insecure as a child. Many of the men who cruised these areas were either in heterosexual relationships or had recently been released from prison and needed a place to stay for the night.

I had become comfortable with these types of pickup spots, but most people would be surprised at the kinds of men that cruised them. I was amazed at the number of married men, black and white, that I met on the strip. I was very uncomfortable about selecting a married man for sexual pleasure because I felt sorry for the women married to him. Of course, I knew many homosexuals who felt married man were the ideal sex partners, feeling that they had conquered the world if they got to seduce one. Their ultimate goal was to have these married men fall in love with them and leave their wives. Also, many homosexuals cruising straight men felt like they were paying them back for all the pain that had been afflicted by them. One thing was understood universally by gay men; as lonely as they were it was rarely an option to have a stable relationship in this lifestyle. In fact, homosexuals count the days of a relationship much like the way we count the first year of a baby's life. If a homosexual relationship was still going on after three months, it was considered a long-term relationship. Homosexual men want relationships badly, but they just don't know how to make them last. Once they fall in love with their "dream man," another handsome hunk can easily cloud their vision and cause the old relationship to end quite quickly.

Regarding the cruise strip, most gay guys spend as long as two hours driving around these spots wasting gallons of gas looking for a quick fix. During my visit to the cruise spot that evening after fitness training, I noticed how different things had become in this area of Atlanta. There were now very high priced condos and lofts starting at $250,000 there. The area was now infested with and upper class white singles and police officers who guarded the area well. But even with all these clear changes, it was also clear that this area was still popular as a gay cruise strip. On this particular night, the guys walking the strip really looked worn down, like heavy drug users and those suffering from HIV/AIDS. However, this did not slow down the traffic for those looking for a good sex fix. Most importantly, the guys on the strip appeared to be very aggressive, some trying to get into cars without being invited. This was an effort to avoid the police who were watching the area, but of course I didn't feel comfortable letting men I didn't know jump in my car. In 1999, men on the strip had become real hustlers and cruising the strip had become all about the Benjamins.

I will never forget the time I did allow a guy in my car that refused to get out unless I gave him money. When I refused he attacked me. I will never forget the afflictions he caused me; I had been hit in my face and although the pain was fierce, I thank God there was a MARTA police officer nearby who was able to arrest him. I was furious and although I did blame myself for being in that spot, I still felt that I didn't deserve to be attacked in that way. I wanted this guy to be prosecuted to the fullest. Upon his arrest, I was instructed to appear in court the next business day which I did in order to make sure that this robber was persecuted. I felt good because I had done something many homosexuals were afraid to do.

On the night I checked out the old cruise spot after my

fitness training, I didn't check it out very long because I knew I had a long ride home. I dreaded that 45-minute ride, so I pushed my car to go about 80 mph on the expressway. Suddenly my car came to an abrupt stop stranding me in the middle of nowhere. I really didn't know the area I was stalled in because I had only been back in Atlanta for about a month, but I knew that I had a good distance to go before I reached home. This could have been a nightmare but although I didn't have transportation for several weeks that followed, God worked things out for me. Praise God! I felt that God had made me take this time out to focus back on him and I began making new living arrangements because I lived too far from the city and my job. I allowed my focus to stay on my job, my new church home, and my fitness training. Although I did seek out homosexuals relationships, I found that many guys didn't take to my newly built up body. The kind of guys that were attracted to me was just the opposite of what I liked. I became really let down because here I had worked very hard to build more muscles and it hadn't counted for much, so I reverted back to my anonymous sex life. This meant visiting the numerous anonymous sex clubs that were on the rise in Atlanta. I had so much turmoil inside because while I was trying to be committed to my walk with God, the city of Atlanta made it very difficult because Atlanta had as many sex clubs as churches, both of which were seeking souls. The most famous sex club was called Serextions which stayed open for business 24 hours a day, 7 days a week. These types of clubs were famous for having chains of establishments all around the city which made competition fierce. These sex clubs won souls throughout the week and on Sundays, while the church only tried to win souls on Sunday; only to lose them again by Sunday evening to these sex clubs. Atlanta was indeed a city that God was not pleased with because people were truly losing their souls to the devil here, due to their perversions. I remember when I lived in Atlanta back in the 1980's it was

109

against the law for sex clubs to exist, so many clubs used fronts that appeared to be legitimate stores selling sex toys. However, in the back of these stores were video booths where illegal sexual activities were actually taking place. Various booths had holes large enough for men to exchange sexual pleasures. By 1999, the openness of these sex clubs in Atlanta made me understand why families began moving to the suburbs, even though many husbands from these same families often snuck back into the city to take part in the illicit activities that Atlanta offered. Atlanta still remains a city that caters well to the homosexual lifestyle.

Learning about these sexual offerings in Atlanta made my Christian journey harder than I could pray help for. This is why I became puzzled as to why churches had not instituted sexual reform programs for homosexuals. Surely, with all the churches around and the power they have, homosexuals can be helped. After witnessing the out of control sexual behaviors within the homosexual community, I could certainly understand why people felt homosexuals deserved to acquire the HIV/AIDS virus. However, take care to remember that many "straight" married men were also involved in these immoral behaviors, yet no other group is condemned in the way that homosexuals are. At any rate, I knew I could not continue to live my life the way I always had, so I continued to seek God through constant fellowshipping and staying in God's word. I recognized that this was the only way for me to obtain a successful life but I still knew I had a war to fight inside. By now I was 35 years old and had begun to find some success at fighting this demon within.

FINDING PURPOSE

Most people stereotype homosexuals, assuming they all belong to certain professions. Most assume that gays are hairstylists, makeup artists, fashion designers, and even drag queens. Although homosexuals are considered to be some of the best and most talented professionals in the entertainment industry, most would put that all aside to gain deliverance from God. At any rate, those in the homosexual community have much broader talents than acknowledged by the mainstream and I was determined to let my talents shine.

Although I grew up with very low self-esteem, I did finally find the courage to believe in myself. I started to build on the confidence of knowing that God loved me and with this confidence I started HUSH Productions. My new company allowed me to work for top celebrities in the entertainment industry. As a fashion producer, I landed assignments working with clients which included Rappers Outkast; Actors Mark Collier and Denzel Washington; Drew Barrymore, Singers Eric Bonet, Tamar Braxton, Johnny Gill, Sister 2 Sister, Keith Sweat and Usher; Gospel Diva Dottie Peoples; Actress AJ Adrienne Johnson; Supermodel Tyson Beckford; Sean John; Publisher Jammie Foster-Brown; and Model Lisa Sweat. The list went on and for me this was a real accomplishment for the little boy who had suffered so many wrongs. Running this leading modeling and production company taught me that love would have nothing to do with whether I made it or not. I had already worked in the entertainment industry but this was more than I had expected. Atlanta had some of the most attractive straight black men seeking stardom. Some gay men thought that they could capitalize on this because it was a sure way to build a nice male clientele base and make easy money. They recognized that people would do anything for stardom, so these bogus gay model agency owners and directors became predators. Although they didn't have anything to offer their recruits, which would be a hard lesson for "wannabe" models to learn, these predators were able to trap unsuspecting hopefuls. Many of these hopefuls were about to lose their souls to the enemy, because the only thing they could offer was overdeveloped muscular bodies but without talent. These were the very things the perpetrator looked for to successfully scam money and sex. Many of these "wannabe" models attended open calls at mainstream model agencies like Elites and LeGlace and were rejected. Those rejected by legitimate agencies would be selected by bogus agencies like Trojans and Golden's Calendars for a price. These untalented aspiring models would be expected to pay hundreds of dollars to the agency. However, had they been selected by a legitimate agency no money would have been required. The perpetrators, which remember, were bogus gay agency owners, knew these men were desperate and they'd believe whatever they were told. It was so easy to convince black "wannabe" male models that they had what it took to make it. All you had to do was feed their egos and they were sold for a price. This game made it really difficult for the smaller legitimate agencies like mine to ultimately recruit them. Some guys had real horror stories about their encounters with bogus modeling business; many being asked to perform sexual favors as part of their modeling duties.

My requirements for male models were not as high as other model agencies. It was very challenging for me to work with well-built male models that I usually contracted for calendar work. I was used to working with female models that I had no sexual attraction for. Besides, my gift had always been in developing and coaching females. My main interest for the calendar was the heterosexual male model, although this project was most difficult because I had never worked this closely with straight male models before. I truly had a real passion for my calendar projects because I wanted to make a positive difference in how male models were being promoted. There had been too much exploiting of black males in the modeling industry, and since most mainstream modeling agencies had no interest in promoting black male models I wanted to do my best to fill this void. That is why it was a blessing to see Tyson Beckford, the most successful black male model, reach the peak of his modeling career and see him last as long as he has. He was the first and only black male supermodel that landed a major modeling contract with the renowned fashion icon, Ralph Lauren. What most black male models didn't know was that modeling was like the rest of the entertainment industry, it was not about who had the most talent but who you knew and whether you were willing to play the game.

FINDING LOVE IN MY LIFE

Also by age 35, I had finally found the love of my life; something I had always wanted. I'd never had anyone to find me attractive in the way my new lover did. Because I preferred very masculine or straight acting men it was difficult to find someone, since truthfully, most homosexuals shared my preference in men. This type just appeared stronger which is not to say that I was weak and could not stand up for myself, but those with the "roughneck" image just didn't seem to care about the opinions of others. Most black gay men feel that being seen with a masculine man keeps their homosexuality a secret better than being seen with a more feminine man. Although many white homosexuals had come out of the closet and spoke about how proud they were of their homosexual lifestyles, most black homosexuals did not share this "out of the closet" sentiment. Very few black homosexuals have gay pride and to be honest most felt it was safer to stay in the closet to avoid unnecessary gay bashing. To be in denial of ones lifestyle is to be in total denial of oneself. Those in denial usually participated in risky and sometimes out of control sexual behaviors and I will admit to being one of those homosexuals who lived in the closet and on the edge. Although many questioned my sexuality because of my effeminate behavior, I chose denial as a response. By now, it should be understood that I hated the constant name-calling and ridiculing that followed me throughout my life, and although I would lie to people about my lifestyle, it would have been better if I had just told the truth since most people already knew the truth about my life. Lying takes so much energy, plus it had caused me to deny who I was. You cannot change who you are unless you are honest about it. At any rate, while getting acquainted with the new love in my life, we were faced with the roles that sometimes defined homosexual relationships. When getting to know one another, gay men will establish early in the relationship whether their partner is a top or bottom. This should be self-explanatory, but in case it isn't I will only say that ideally a gay male couple is made up of one male who is a top while the other is a bottom. So, if a relationship progressed to intimacy, the question became, "Are you top or bottom." This determines compatibility in the relationship. In earlier years, when I started practicing the lifestyle, most men just got together to enjoy the company of one another, but things have changed within the dating scene pushing homosexual dynamics to another level.

Having a committed relationship with a man was a form of validation for me, and I was having trouble believing that the relationship I finally found myself in was real. This caused me to have many conversations with God regarding this newfound love in my life. I prostrated before God in prayer, asking him if he could accept and bless my new homosexual relationship; a stretch since the Bible clearly rejects any such union. Many nights I had prayed for the life most people had and I tried desperately to want a relationship with a woman. This honestly was one of my constant prayers, but I had to then ask myself if I wanted a relationship with a woman because it was more acceptable to the world or did I truly desire it. Here is what I came to understand: although in my heart I certainly wanted to be intimate with a woman, it certainly would never have satisfied my flesh. So, I chose love with my new friend and I could not have been any happier. I entered in not expecting our relationship to last long because as I mentioned before, homosexual relationships usually ended quickly. But, I felt relaxed in his presence even though I had never felt comfortable around black men before. It was wonderful to be treated with the love he expressed towards me.

My lover who was an island born man from Barbados had a beautiful accent, which definitely didn't hurt when it came to adding something special to our relationship. Whenever he spoke to me his strong masculine voice sounded sweet to my ears. From our first sexual encounter he was very romantic and obviously knew how to please. I had never experienced this kind of romance before from any guy I had encountered. This was a relationship which was well overdue in my life, and it surprised me to learn later that my newfound partner had never been in a sexual relationship with a man before. I was really excited when he told me that he had never felt this way about anyone, because no man had ever honestly expressed this to me. This was clearly a sign that things were headed in the right direction. I felt as if I were floating on cloud nine with every day starting and ending like the first day we met. I was waited on hand and foot and was given attention I had never experienced. Finally, I was being treated like a valued person; love is something all human beings want even homosexuals. Our relationship continued in a positive direction for an unheard of two years, and because I was living the life that so many gay men wanted much hatred was directed at me by outsiders. I was used to this, however, and although I stayed with my lover many nights during the week, I felt that I wanted to be even closer to him so we discussed living together. That is why it seemed so sudden when one day my lover expressed that he had a change of heart about us living together, and he even seemed to be reconsidering our relationship. I knew enough to know that this was usually the behavior of either a bi-sexual or heterosexual man who started feeling stress about being involved in a homosexual relationship. It was as if he had all of a sudden thought about the lifestyle he was living and wanted to begin denying it.

So many times my lover spoke of getting custody of his six-year-old son who lived with his mother in Florida, and of course I encouraged him to pursue actions to gain custody. Within months, his son had moved to Atlanta, a move that caused our relationship to quickly begin to sour. His son and I both competed for his time and attention, but I should have known I could never compete against anyone's child and my attempt ended in defeat. I began to feel angry at the world again; a world I had not hated since I met him. I blamed the world for my misery because it was the world's view of homosexuality that had caused him to rethink our relationship. I also hated the homosexual world for not embracing our union, because their support may have given him some sense of acceptance from somewhere. Never again would I experience this type of relationship, and I am not sure if it was even a good thing that I got the chance to experience it at all. After our breakup I found myself spending more time in church and drawing even closer to God.

CHURCH WOMEN

I often listened to church women talk about their future dream men. I enjoyed listening to them because they never seemed to be speaking from a world of reality when they spoke of the kind of men they hoped to meet and marry. This was funny to me because most church women had not been in relationships for many years, at least that is what I got from their conversations. Because I have experienced the challenges of staying celibate, I was surprised that so many of them professed to have mastered it.

I personally never had a problem praising God in church on Sunday mornings, only to sleep with men that same night. I had a lot of difficulty abstaining from sexual activities because I have always been involved with sex willingly and unwillingly. Many church women confided in me and confirmed that abstaining was not as easy as the average church woman seemed to project. I know there has to be some truth to this because many single church women end up pregnant, and it's odd but when they do they are rarely condemned. Rather the births of their babies are celebrated, which is clearly a contradiction to God's values as is the countless unborn babies who are never talked about. As a homosexual I always saw these contradictions by churchgoers as unfair.

I spent much time with women after church, joining them for dinner and it seemed that after they stopped gossiping it was clear that most didn't have a life outside of church. They didn't really believe in biblical teachings nor have much faith in the path they had chosen. More than anything, I would want churchgoers to know that even though I have seen faults in them everyone has a right to God's grace and mercy, even those struggling with homosexuality. Being a witness to the many flaws I saw in Christians, I still desired to seek God.

THE NAKED TRUTH

Ultimately, I found a church in Atlanta where I felt somewhat grounded, but for some reason I began to judge and gossip about my new pastors and God didn't like it. I left the church and began wandering to different churches, still talking about my new pastors. God's word warns us not to put our mouths on his prophets and as a result of backbiting my pastors, my life took a turn that I will never forget. Everything in my life crumpled, from my relationships and my business ventures, to my health. Love left me, business opportunities failed, and the thing that I dreaded had finally came home to roost. Illness knocked on my door. It seemed like overnight when I began to feel ill to the point where I was visiting the doctor's office once a week which for me was a rarity. I had never been this sick before but now I was experiencing the symptoms that HIV/AIDS patients reported feeling. My body was wracked with pain and I was experiencing sore throats, high fevers, sweats, continuous coughing, and worst of all the signature rapid weight loss. One day, after six months of this torture I became fearful because I just could not breathe and I finally gave in and drove myself to one of Atlanta's community hospitals. After performing an x-ray, and finding pneumonia, the doctor hit me with the news. I began to seek God like never before, repenting of all my sins especially against my pastors. As I continued to cry out, I thought about how I had talked about and mistreated them. The doctors told me that I had the virus, but I initially refused to accept what the doctors were telling me. I just prayed and prayed and asked my true friends to pray for me. These friends knew how to fight Satan with prayers which focused on spiritual warfare, and together we sent up prayers of deliverance on my behalf.

Tragically, as it turned out, I was not just HIV positive but I had contracted full-blown AIDS with a cd4 count of three. Anyone knowing anything about this awful disease will tell you that it is humanly impossible to be alive with such a low number. A normal person would have a cd4 count ranging 800-1200. I did not have a full understanding about what cd4's were, but my doctor explained that they are the white cells (balanced with the red cells) which help protect the immune system. The immune system is the body's system that fights various infections which attack the body. Without the defense of the white blood cells, an infection could take over the body and cause death. When a person's cd4 falls under a 200 count the person is medically labeled as having full-blown AIDS.

After learning all I could about AIDS, I was able to accept what was happening to me and I knew in my heart that I had to see my pastors as well as others that I had offended before I left this earth. I knew I needed to ask for their forgiveness as a true sign of repentance. While struggling with my illness I had much time to reflect over my life and identify those who I had wronged. I certainly did not feel good about my past, and I also began to reflect on those things that were important and those that were not. I recalled those celebrities who I met and worked with, all of whom were very wealthy with the material possessions of a lifetime, but because of my illness I understood that nothing they could have given me would have been able to fulfill or save my life at that point. Only God could fulfill and save my life completely.

My biggest fear was in knowing that my mother would not be able to handle losing another child. I was okay with death but I wanted to be completely at peace with God and with those he had put in and over my life. I had always tried to be a spiritual person, although I did not always know what that really meant. I had come to believe that being spiritual meant belonging to the perfect church, but I learned later from a show aired on *Oprah* that spirituality had nothing to do with attending church, it is the meaning you bring to your life. The spiritual question is: "In the end, did you accomplish those things that really mattered?" I knew in my heart that I had not accomplished the things God had desired for me to do. During my illness God sent a beautiful angel back into my life named Melissa. I met Melissa while living in Washington, D.C., and although we had lost contact with one another when I moved to Atlanta, God placed us back together during my illness. Melissa called me every day and night, helping to comfort me through this most difficult battle in my life. She prayed with me and comforted me through my pain. Although Melissa wasn't familiar with AIDS, she researched my symptoms and began to understand those things that I was suffering with. She never pointed her finger at me or belittled me because of my homosexual lifestyle. The power of love and the people who give it with their true heart are priceless.

It was a long road to recovery taking almost three long years for me to get back my physical and mental health. This was mainly because of the severity of my illness and the tremendous amount of weight I lost due to the PCP pneumonia I acquired as a symptom of the AIDS. I not only suffered physically but I also suffered a financial setback as well, because I was no longer able to operate my entertainment business and keep income flowing in. Prior to my illness I had gotten used to having financial stability that included eating out nightly and living in a luxury I had become accustomed to. My meetings with celebrities and industry executives came to a halt as well. My life as a successful executive became only a memory. It felt good, however, to hold on to those memories of my high profile life, because it was those memories that helped me during my recovery. I had wonderful memories which included being teased by R&B singer Keith Sweat, who I worked very closely with helping to launch his new clothing line. He had taught me to never let people see me sweat.

As I worked through my recovery, I allowed myself to focus on these types of friendships and I could honestly say that I truly enjoyed working closely with Keith who I had come to admire for his longevity in the music business. I began to understand that Keith survived working in the impossible entertainment arena because he had a close relationship with God. I admired this most about him and his example help propel me even faster through recovery. Keith and I had once attended the same church and I found comfort in remembering the day he went to the altar and turned his life over to God. I remember that was considered a big deal because even the *Atlanta Journal Constitution* wrote a huge article about his newly found life as a Christian. The article talked about Keith making a confession to end his music and entertainment career because that old lifestyle was contradictive to the Gospel of Christ and the word of God. Unfortunately, even he found it too difficult to resist the devil and give up the glitz, glamour, and lucrative financial deals, of his old lifestyle. No matter, I still considered it an honor and blessing to have worked with such an influential R&B artist, because as I faced recovery I pooled from the fond memories I had with Keith and those I had come to find joy being around.

I had established a wonderful working relationship with Mr. Brown, the program director at WVEE V-103 radio station. My company had also partnered with CBS infinity broadcasting WVEE (V-103) the number one radio station in Atlanta. V-103 had the power to make any black owned company number one because of their continuous number one ranking amongst Atlanta listeners. This was the one thing about Atlanta that I had come to enjoy; it's rising population of over 4 million people. Working with a number one radio station got my company noticed all over the city and created opportunities for doors to be opened in other major cities as well. Honestly, I was amazed at what God had done for me and my business. However, as the Bible says, there is a time and season for everything and due to my illness my season was about to end abruptly.

The one positive thing about working in the entertainment business was that it offered financial stability to those who knew the ins and outs of the business. I was able to establish key friendships with other "down low" homosexuals in the business who had much more clout than I did and who were able to help keep me up on the latest news and gossip in the business. Most importantly they were able to get me VIP passes to the hottest celebrity events I would otherwise not be privy to. The one thing homosexuals offered to the entertainment business was their creative talents. Even heterosexuals admired this about us. Although it was common knowledge that homosexual entrepreneurs were not welcomed in this industry, even those who made that rule had to admit that there were times when they needed our help.

I learned very quickly that the entertainment world was no place for the weak, but was for those who knew how to get what they wanted at any cost, and I had certainly known what I wanted from the entertainment world even if it meant I had to lose my soul to the DEVIL. I came in the game with no experience and no mentor to teach me how the business worked but I learned the game and caught on very quickly. I refused to do anything harmfully illegal which meant I didn't get ahead as fast as I could have, but I learned the ropes well. It took me a moment but I soon learned that celebrities usually didn't mind spending lots of money on anyone who came recommended or could promise them great results, both of which described me. I enjoyed the fame that came with this life but I wasn't very much prepared for a long tenure in the entertainment field. My illness proved to be the very thing that cut my stint with this industry shorter than I would have hoped.

I had given my life over to the devil for things that didn't honor God. I knew in many ways that I didn't like how I had to lie and cheat for my next contract. Although I had a very close relationship with God, I had begun letting it slip just before the onset of my illness. God had to show me that this was a business that he was not pleased with, because the entertainment world required much lying, stealing, and sometimes killing of souls, just to be successful in it. In other words, in order to be successful in this world your soul was required and I, like everyone else, played the game ready to lose mine.

Once I became ill and had lost everything, I sat in my hospital room and had over two weeks to think about my life. I had no time to play the blame game because my life was on the line. I could not afford to waste one moment thinking about what I had lost because I had to put all my energy on fighting for my life. When I was admitted into a community hospital here in Atlanta, I arrived not in a limo but gasping for air due to a lack of oxygen flowing through my lungs. It felt as if my lungs had collapsed, and to add to that pain was my fear at being in a community hospital because truthfully I had heard that this particular hospital had lost many patients due to the fact that patient care was provided by medical interns rather than experienced doctors. However, with my medical condition so poor and my money very low I could not afford to care about whom was treating my condition. At the time of my admittance to the emergency room speaking was very difficult. Because my chance of survival was slim, I was not made to wait in the overcrowded emergency room. I remember thinking that I never thought the day would come when I would need life support to remain alive. This was something I saw people go through on television or while visiting friends in the hospital. But I was about to be put on oxygen support for several days to help support my breathing, because I was too weak to breathe on my own. I was also put in isolation away from other patients in order to protect me from any additional harm that might be caused by airborne diseases.

After accepting the reality of my diagnosis, I had some real decisions to make that included calling my mother in Daytona Beach and my sister Vanessa in Memphis to inform them of my illness. It would take a lot of strength and guts for me to call my mother who had already lost two children to AIDS. How would I tell her that another of her children was in critical condition suffering from the disease that had plagued our family? I felt my news would tear her apart, not to mention that it could have even caused her to have a heart attack. I really had to consider these things before sharing this kind of news with her over the telephone. My mother and I had always stayed in contact with each other by talking on the phone several times a week. Being in the hospital meant she would be unable to reach me. I prayed that my breathing would return to a normal state so that I might call her, but I knew it would be days before that could happen. My prayer became, please God let me survive.

When my breathing had finally returned to normal, I called my mother and told her that I was out of town and I would contact her as soon as I returned. After several more days had passed I began feeling a little better, and decided to call my mother again to tell her the truth about my situation. Knowing my mother as well as I did, I knew that she already suspected something was wrong, but I still tried to talk myself out of telling her what was really going on with me. In the end I decided it was time to start being honest with myself and others, so I opted to tell her exactly what was going on. As I began to tell her my news there was a strange silence on her end of the telephone. When I asked if she was still there, a loud burst of screams and cries came from my mother's end of the phone. She began yelling, "God why are you doing this to me?" I yelled for my mother to please try to calm down because I was going to be fine. Honestly, I really didn't know what would become of me but my spirit spoke to me softly and told me that I would be fine if I pressed myself toward healing. After my mother calmed down, she told me that she knew something was wrong, because her spirit had told her several days before when she had tried to contact me. Although my mother wasn't a regular churchgoer, she had more faith than most churchgoers I knew so I knew her faith would carry her through this crisis. I hung up with that assurance and began concentrating on my health.

I no longer looked the same because of the tremendous amount of weight I had lost, but I knew that I had to depend on God to give me strength to make it. I recall my doctors during rounds coming in my room with sad faces, as if to say that they had done all they could do for me. Every morning around 7:00 a.m., I would get myself together and put a big smile on my face so when my doctors entered the room they might be convinced that I was doing better and would agree to let me go home. However, each morning when they entered my room the look on their faces let me know that I was not doing as well as I thought. Even though they spoke in codes around me, so I would not know the severity of my case, I would think positive because I understood the power of God. When they left my room they sometimes patted me on my head shaking their heads as if my impending fate was sealed. Refusing to buy into their doubt I kicked my faith into fifth gear, because I was determined that I was going to make it through this ordeal no matter what. Although I recognized that I was against impossible odds, I knew I served a mighty God who had the power to see me through anything.

Still, I did have some weak points and fear seeped in. During these times I refused to go to sleep because I was afraid that I would not wake up. Sometimes I just stayed awake because I didn't want the enemy to put the thought of death in my head in dreams. Although this was the first time I would desperately need God for deliverance, I trusted and believed God's word that promised healing to the believer. I had spent too many years studying and learning about the power of God for me to faint now. I also understood that prayer would play a huge factor in my complete recovery, so I contacted my friends and church family and had them intercede on my behalf. I began praying to God without ceasing, asking him to comfort my mother and also give me the strength I needed to get through yet another battle in my life. I remembered that I had already come to understand that when faced with a struggle it did not belong to me, it belonged to God, so I tried very hard to turn my cares over to him in order to avoid the stress of worrying.

The next person I would need to contact was my older sister Vanessa whom I had come to love, but hadn't spoken to in quite awhile since we both kept very busy schedules. Vanessa by now was a homemaker and mother of two small children, while I was busy chasing entertainment executives. Vanessa and I had a unique relationship because while we both loved one another, we also acted very much alike. Because the outside world had been the source of so much of our pain, we both tended to guard our hearts from it. Being so much alike, in that we grew up feeling alone in our struggles, Vanessa and I had a unique way of expressing our love towards one another. However, my sister's struggle ended when she married the man of her dreams, one who obviously felt that she was the most important woman in the world to him. I was even surprised when she began living the Cinderella life that most little girls only dreamed of. Vanessa was a lot more outgoing and was very much an extrovert who enjoyed the company of people. I, on the other hand, was a true introvert. So, while I knew my sister had faced many struggles, I also knew that what she had gone through was nothing like what I had endured living the life of homosexual.

My older sister didn't have a problem with speaking her mind, while I usually chose to keep most of what I thought hidden deep inside myself; this didn't change until I became much older. When I learned to speak my mind, in my later years, it was usually prompted by anger caused by trying to justify my existence. My sister and I lived very different lives. She loved sports and was very good at them, while I was into dancing and doing more feminine things. I often enjoyed the time my older sister and I spent together because she loved and spoiled me like no one else did. She realized how different I was even as a child but like my mother, Vanessa felt very helpless as to how to help me. Still, she also supported and loved me unconditionally. I relished the times we spent together, but when she became married with children it changed our relationship drastically. I often hated to think about her being away from me, and it sometimes brought me to tears because we no longer had the closeness that defined our special relationship. I will never forget the day that Vanessa got married and how I cried like a baby as she walked down the aisle toward her new prince. That was probably the second saddest day of my life because although I had not lost her to death as I had my baby sister, I still felt a tremendous loss because I our relationship would never been the same.

I certainly didn't know how Vanessa would handle the news about my illness, but I began to think about her family and how close and supportive they were with each other. I loved Vanessa's daughter, Ashley, so much because in many ways she reminded me of my baby sister. Ashley was the sweetest and smartest little girl, who always showed me how much she loved me as her uncle. Both my sister's children had the privilege of attending private schools from as early as pre-school, which was something I never experienced. I had always thought it was a blessing to be able to attend private school because children there were usually protected from the verbal abuse and cruelty other children could inflict. I knew firsthand of the self-esteem issues that such abuse could cause at an early age. As a small child, Ashley showed no signs of acquiring self-esteem problems, and her very strong personality was complimented by being outspoken as well. My sister was very protective of her children and I couldn't blame her because of the molestations I had suffered at the hands of strangers. Ashley's love for me showed how innocent children were and how they loved without conditions. I loved how Ashley would remind me of the little boy inside myself, making me wish I could return to my childhood and experience my young life in the same way she and her brother had.

Although I knew I had a deadly disease, Ashley would never know, and would therefore not treat me any differently than she always had. I knew I could always count on love from my niece, and I looked forward to seeing her each year during the Christmas holidays. I thoroughly treasured this festive time that I spent with Vanessa and her family, and because their home was very accommodating for what remained of our dwindling family, Vanessa offered to have us spend Christmas with her and her family every year.

Vanessa had definitely overcome the odds and was living a wonderful life. She had married a very successful computer programmer, which allowed her to live a middle-class lifestyle with a home that I had always desired for my baby sister. In fact, Vanessa's home reminded me in many ways of the home of a celebrity I once worked for. Spending the holidays with my sister and her family allowed us to forget about the pain caused by the deaths of our siblings and father.

While preparing how to tell Vanessa about my illness, I was glad that she had the support of her family. We had lost so many siblings over the years, and because Vanessa was my oldest sister—the one who had always protected me from the cruelty of the world—I didn't know how she would react to my news. Even if she did not approve of the homosexual lifestyle I lived, she never showed any signs of it because of the unconditional love she always displayed toward me. Knowing this, I decided it best to go ahead and just make the call to her, telling her the truth about what I was facing. When she initially heard my news Vanessa started crying and took the bad news really hard, however, I was able to encourage her not to lose control. Just like I knew she would, Vanessa began asking what I needed and if I needed her to come to see about me. Because of my strong independent nature I told her I would be fine and encouraged her not to come. In truth, I would have loved it if she had just shown up anyway, and I often imagined that one morning I'd wake up to find that she had come to surprise me. This is something my baby sister often did when I got into trouble and needed help getting out of it. I knew that Vanessa would have come but she had just returned to the workforce after being home for seven long years caring for her children. Besides that, I knew that her husband had suffered a job loss due to the economy and they could not spare the money for her to come at that time.

The many days I spent in the hospital, I thought hard about how I had struggled to exist in a world that wanted nothing to do with the little boy who had been molested and who grew up to live the promiscuous life of a homosexual. But even in the lonely life I had lived there was always a place I could go to find peace and restoration. That place would be in God. I knew as a child that God loved me and had shown great mercy towards me, yet I had to suffer because as an adult I chose bad paths rather than choosing God. As I lay in that hospital bed, I realized that I could either build my life on hatred and play the blame game or I could choose to forgive my abusers and be FREE in Jesus. It was during those days in the hospital, fighting for my life, that I understood God was using my illness to bring me to the point of understanding I had always searched for. You see, my hospital visitors were few and telephone calls were rare. Many of my friends and church members had informed me that they were praying for me but unfortunately didn't have time to fit me into their busy schedules as far as visiting me. God was showing me so much that I had to see in order to understand that I needed to lean solely on him for comfort and deliverance.

July 4, 2000, was another day that served to show that it was time for me to put my total trust in God rather than others. Like with most Fourth of Julys, my friends were having a cookout at the home of Keith Sweat. I lay in the hospital wishing for someone to come by to see about me. One of my best friends really disappointed me when he told me that he couldn't leave the cookout to come and visit. Desperate, I made another telephone call to someone I had loved very much and asked him to come by to visit me, but he stated that he could not come by either. I pleaded and begged him to bring me something to drink just so I could see him and have some company. While he did come by to deliver the drinks, he stayed only a few moments explaining that he had to leave to go see about his son whom he left over a neighbor's house. This is when I realized that I was really alone and I mean really alone. It was then that I began trusting solely in God and fighting for my life. It was finally clear that at that point there was only me and God.

After I was released from the hospital, I had to take drastic steps to regain my health, but it would not be without yet another stay at the hospital. My savings had dwindled to almost nothing and I was forced to move out of my upscale Buckhead apartment in Atlanta. This caused me undue stress which caused my health to fail again landing me back in the hospital. Because of the lack of rest I had received upon my first return home, I had a reoccurrence of the PCP pneumonia and a body temperature of over 103 degrees. This bout was fierce and the symptoms seemed as if they would never let up. Being readmitted to the hospital was short-lived, as I could not stop

THE CRY OF A LITTLE BOY

thinking about the fact that I had nowhere to live so I made the harsh decision to walk out of the hospital with an IV still in my arm. This meant that should I have needed to be readmitted to that same hospital, they could refuse me because I had broken one of their policies when I left without informing anyone. When I walked out of the hospital I was sweating uncontrollably and was in terrible pain. I returned to my car and began driving around the city concerned about my homeless situation. This was the time I should have been more concerned with my health, but I new God was with me. I could not get anyone to help me; not my friends, family, or church members. Finally, a sister of one of my best friends came to my rescue and allowed me to move into her basement apartment. This is one of the sweetest women I had ever met; a member of my church who opened her arms to me. I knew this was a blessing from God because not only was Delores providing me with shelter, she was also a nurse who kept her eye on me during my recovery. Most importantly, she resembled my mother when I was a little boy which brought me so much comfort. In many ways I wanted to resent my mother for not coming to see about me at a time that I needed her most. However, even though this was the most devastating time of my life, I had to understand that she thought I was dying and could not bear to see me in the condition I was in. Knowing all that she had already gone through with this disease it was easy for me to forgive her for not coming.

Through my illness I also found it easy to forgive all those who had stolen my innocence by raping and molesting me as a child. I forgave those who so cruelly teased me throughout my life's journey, and I even forgave myself for the choices I made that did not honor God. Finally, I asked God to forgive me for all the times I walked past him to get to sin. When I think about homosexuality now, I have to say that I truly don't believe anyone is born gay. It wasn't that God could not change me all along; I just refused to allow him to take total control of my life and take away my fleshly desires. When I think about those things that fuel my life, I can't help thinking about a recent interview with boxing champion Mike Tyson who stated that the world should experience some of the pain it inflicts on others. I wholeheartedly agree with this because no one has a right to judge others. Thank God that he is both judge and jury.

I fully understand the purpose of God in my life now; and recognize that it was only he who could permanently remove my struggles. I also know that only God could mend my brokenness and put me back together to a state of wholeness. God allows me to speak to him when I am at my weakest, through prayer and meditation, and I've learned that it is only God who can forgive me of my past sins and remove the hurts of my childhood that ultimately carried over into my adulthood. Although I gave my life to God over ten years ago, it took lingering on the brink of death for me to finally see the blessing of my life. Now at age 40, my damaged spirit has been made whole through God's forgiveness; something no man, woman, or child, could offer me. I no longer search for peace in people, places, or material gains. God is my peace.

I know now that in the past the devil just sat back and laughed at me, because he knew that although I had joined the church I had not made a real connection with God; meaning I didn't really value the true meaning and blessing of salvation. Although I desperately wanted this change in my life, I honestly did not believe it could ever happen. I know now that I have always felt the presence of God in my life trying to deliver me. I always felt the presence of his angels guarding and protecting me even while being abused as a child. I also know that God had the power to deliver me all along but I had to truly desire it. Instead, I continued to get sidetracked by the world, church politics, and acting on what my flesh desired. After my near-death experience, and prematurely losing my loved ones, I know that it is time for me to stop "playing church" and answer the call that God has placed on my life.

Over the last two years, I have been preparing myself for his call which is to help others who are hurting and struggling with homosexuality. I have also decided to write my story to expose the naked truth about the myths and truths of what it means to be homosexual in the church and in the world. I realize that I had to strip myself of everything in order to heal and tell my story. My new purpose in life is to use love to help people be the best that they can be; that alone would mean success to me. Although I have done a lot of disappointing things in my life, my heart knows now that God has always loved me. Today, church is very therapeutic for me, and I have begun to truly understand that Jesus, the Son of God, REALLY died to redeem My sins. I think how worthy he must find me in order to make me a sacrifice like that. Through prayer, attending church, and continuing to do those things God requires of me, life is more worthwhile. Still, I live every day as if it is my last, by touching the lives of others in positive ways and keeping my heart on God.

Today, my virus remains at an undetectable status. People of all walks of life seek me for fitness and health advice. These are the two things along with God that helped put me on my road to recovery from nearly dying of AIDS. It was important that I didn't give in to the fear or physical demand the virus was taking on my body. Training all my life helped me to remain disciplined during my battle which I believe accounted for the progress in my healing. I feel blessed to be a living testimony of God's grace and the will he has given me to survive. I encourage everyone who reads my story, especially those suffering from a life-threatening disease to take back control of your life by getting healthy through fellowshipping with God, exercising, and eating healthy. Making this investment may save your life.

I give GOD ALL THE GLORY for my life because only God and I knew how sick I really was. Each day I wake I thank and praise him for his continuing mercy. I choose now to live a life that reflects God more fully and continuously honors him for the mercy he has extended to me by giving me back my life. I refuse to allow people and things of this world to put me back in chains or shackles, and today I declare to the world that I have been set FREE. I have taken total authority over my life through the power of God and the sacrifice of Christ who died so I might be saved. Like anyone who struggles from an addiction, my homosexual desires will always be within, but they will no longer be an active part of my existence. No more depression engulfs my spirit. My self-esteem has risen to an all-time high. I have a new positive direction because God has laid out his plan for my life which is for me to use my experiences to help save others who are dying in sin. My journey has been a difficult one yet I look to the future with the fullness of joy. Although I will never forget that brave little boy who was forced to endure so many abuses, I take care to thank God with everything in my being for allowing him to find peace by Overcoming "The Struggle."

Printed in the United States
71125LV00003BA/114

9 781413 721744